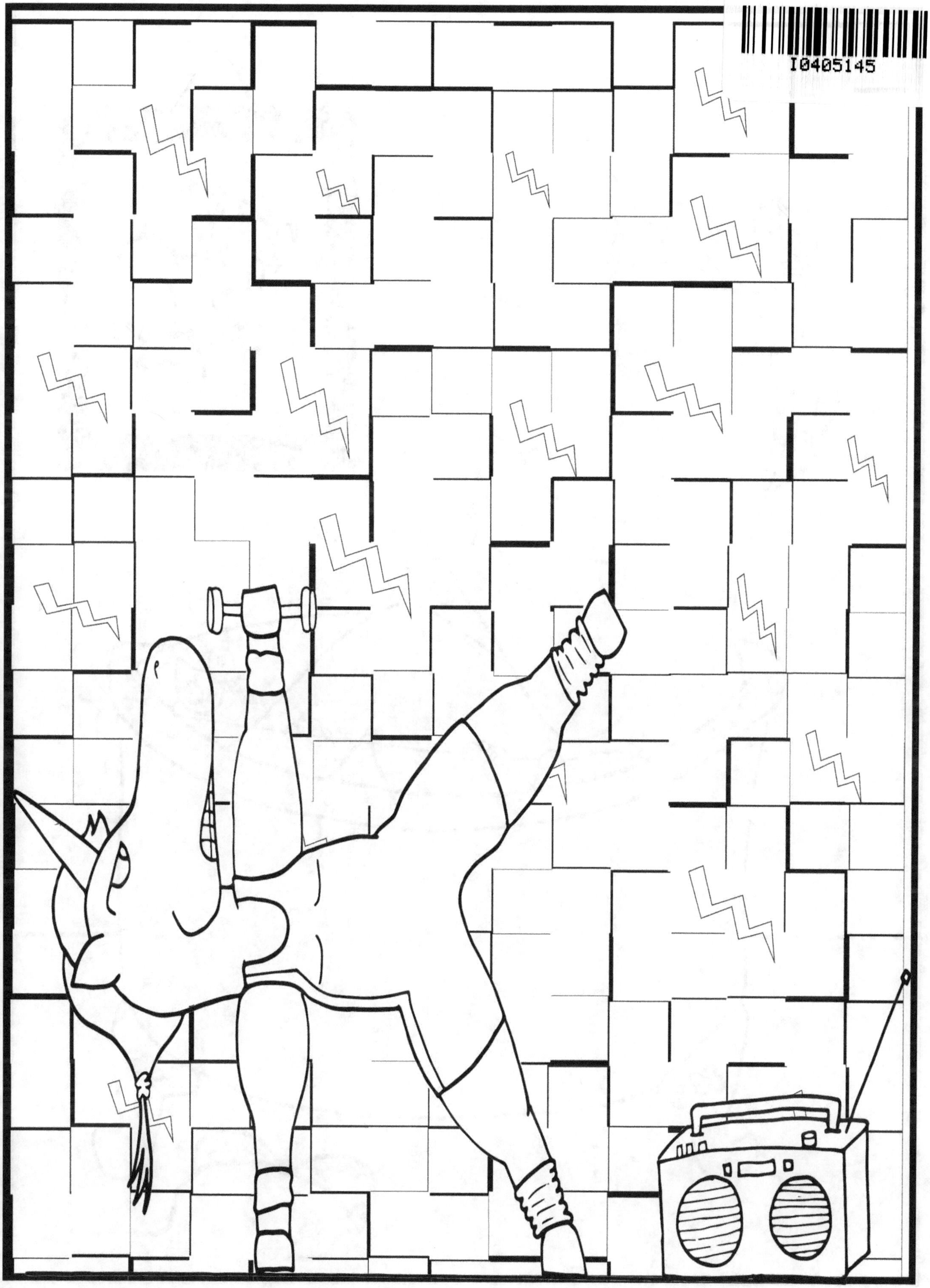

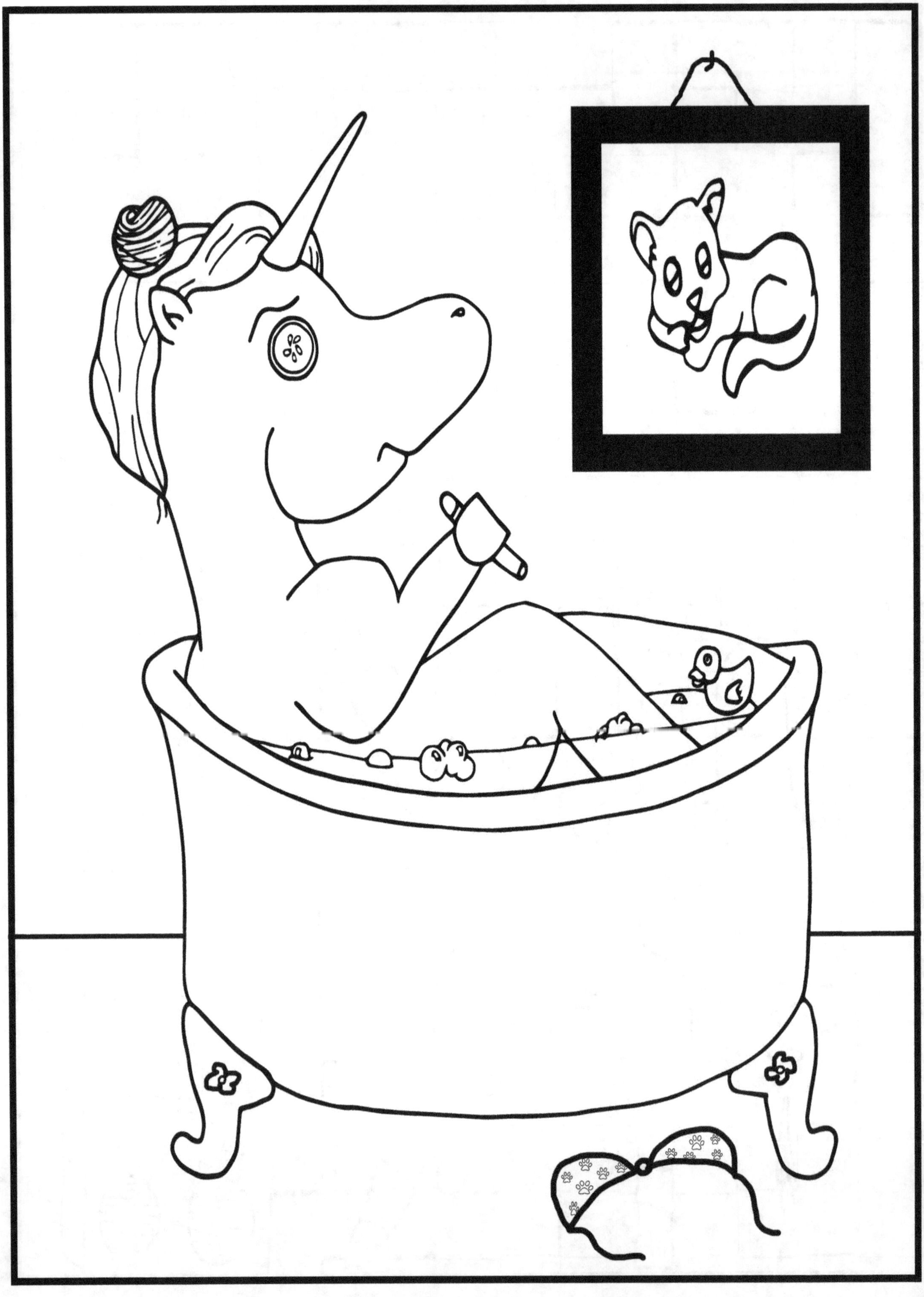

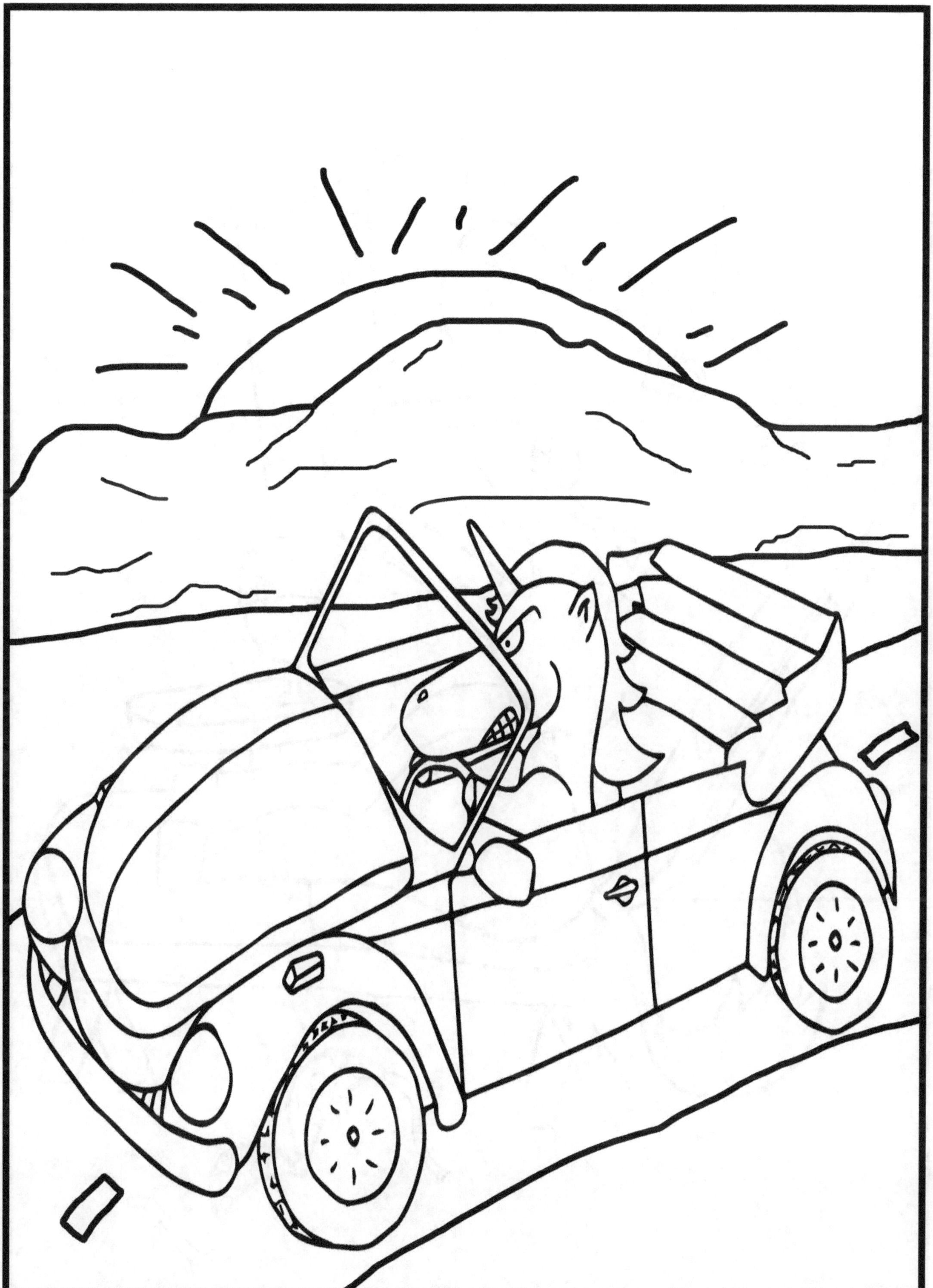

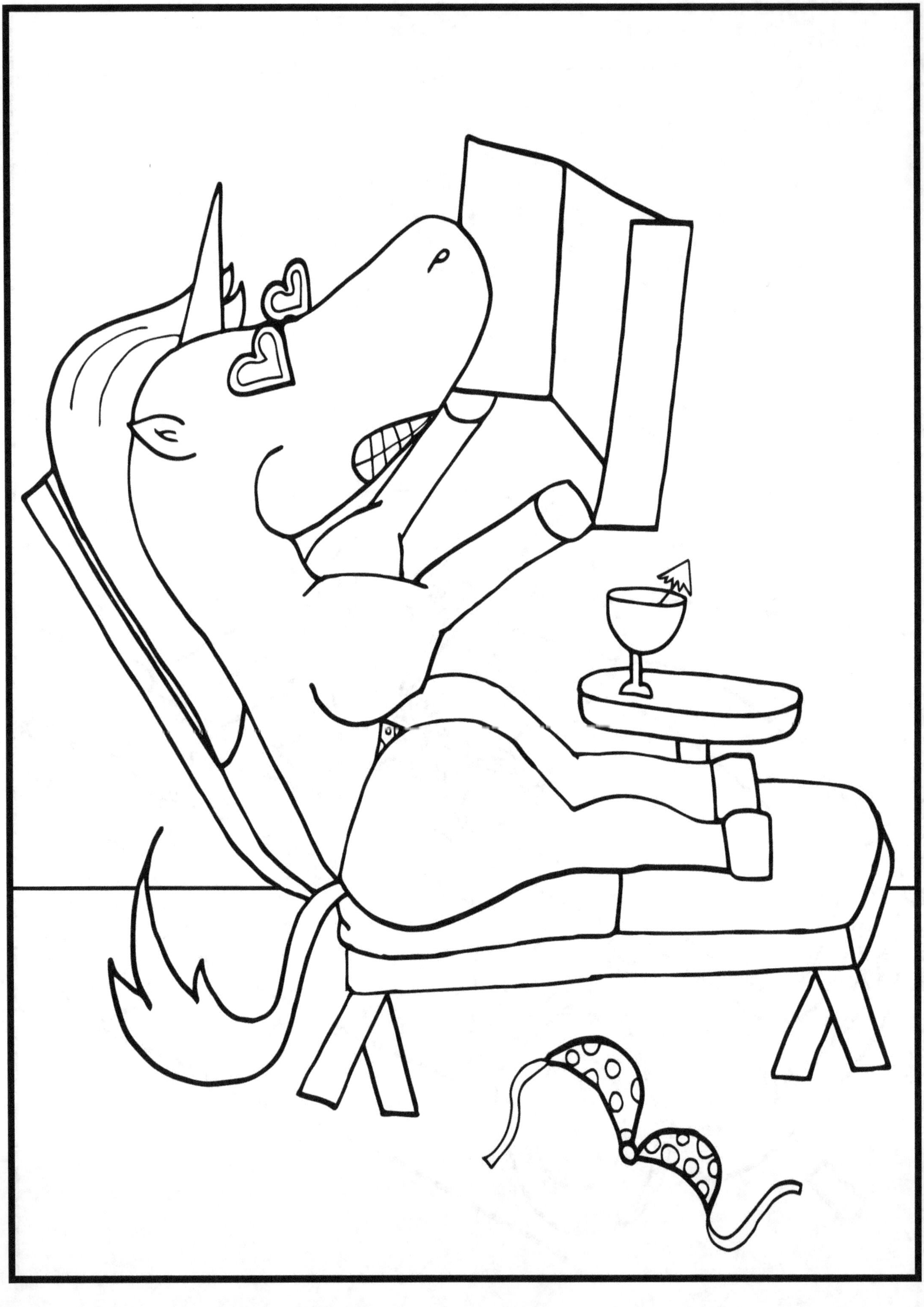

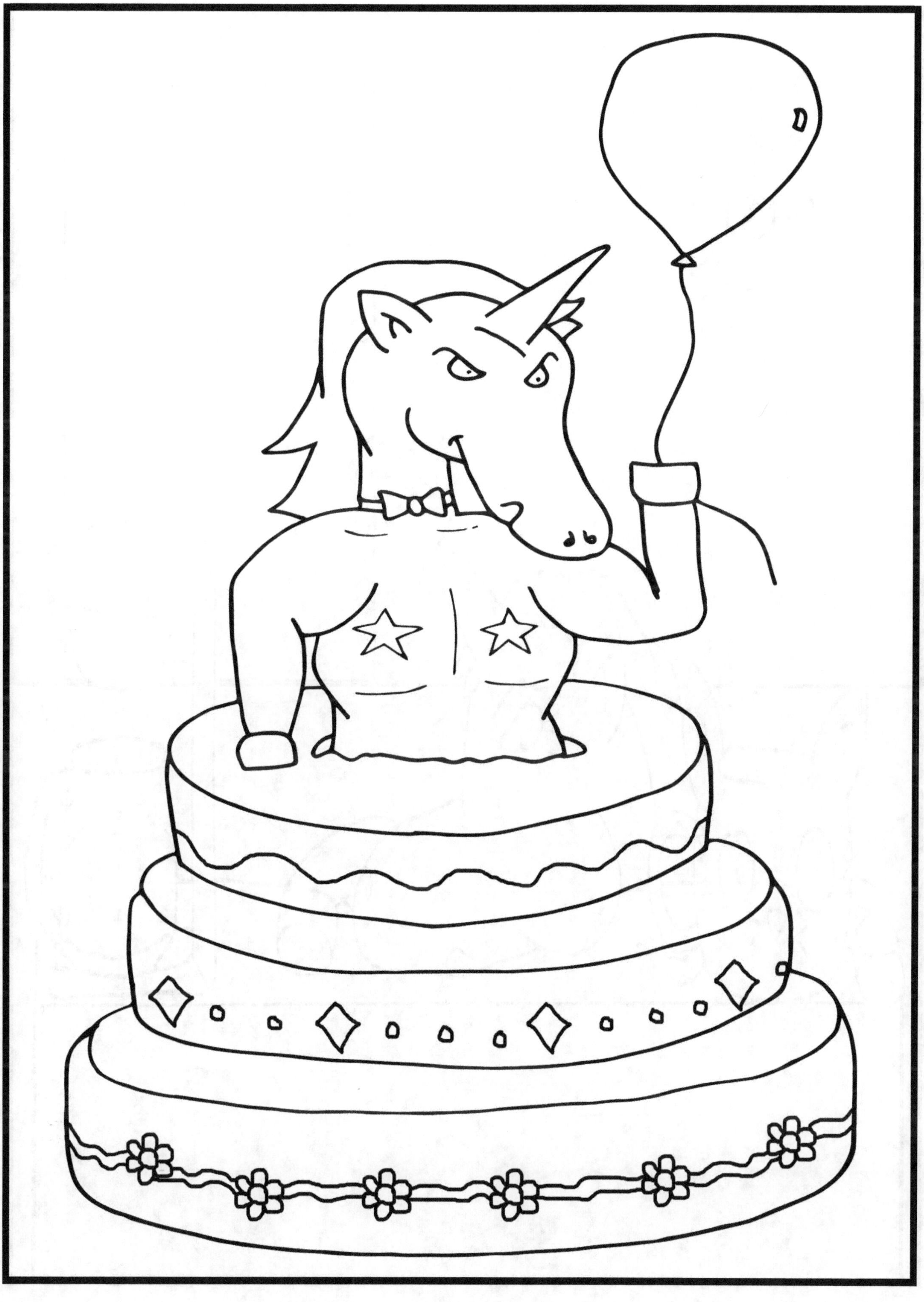

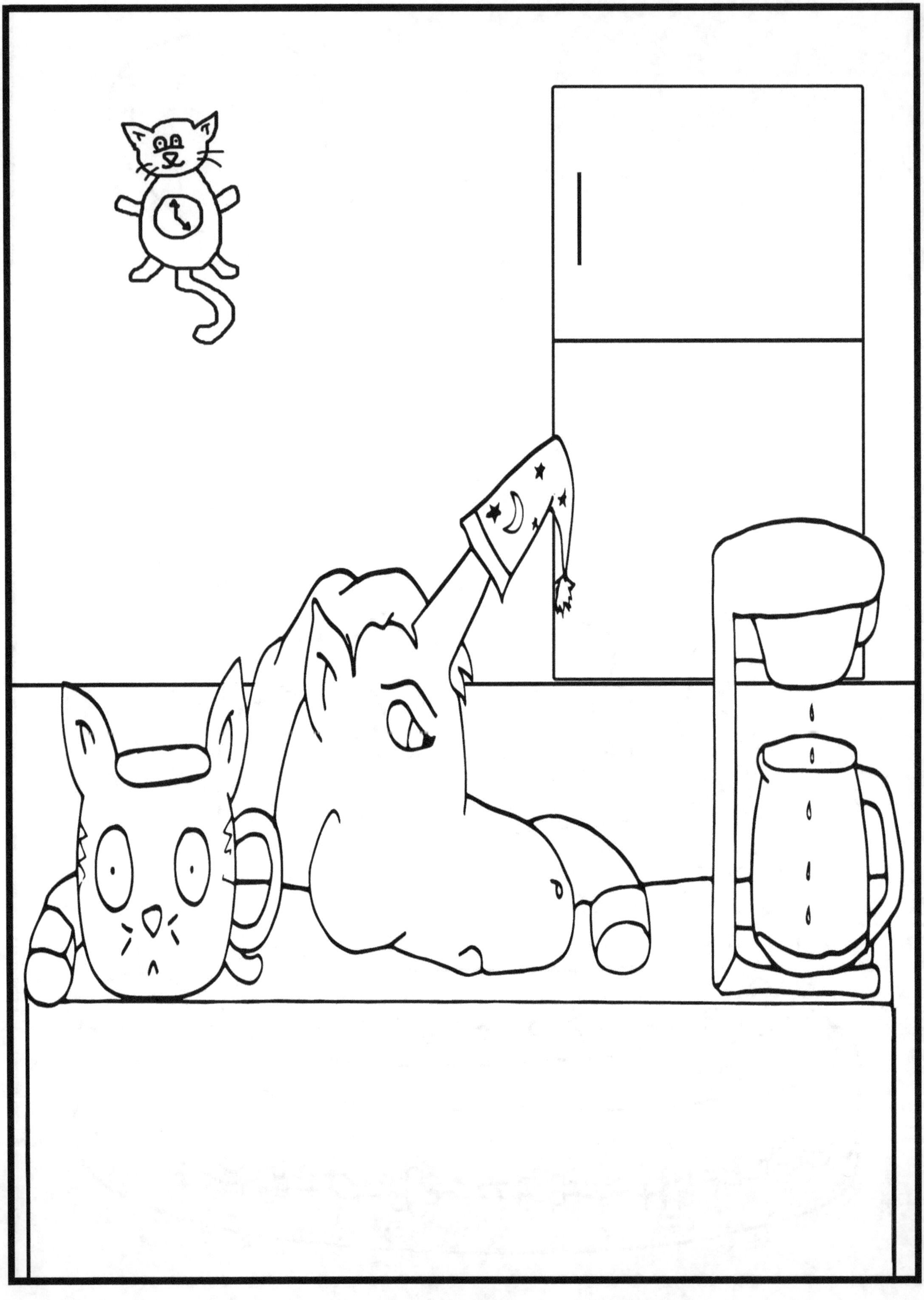

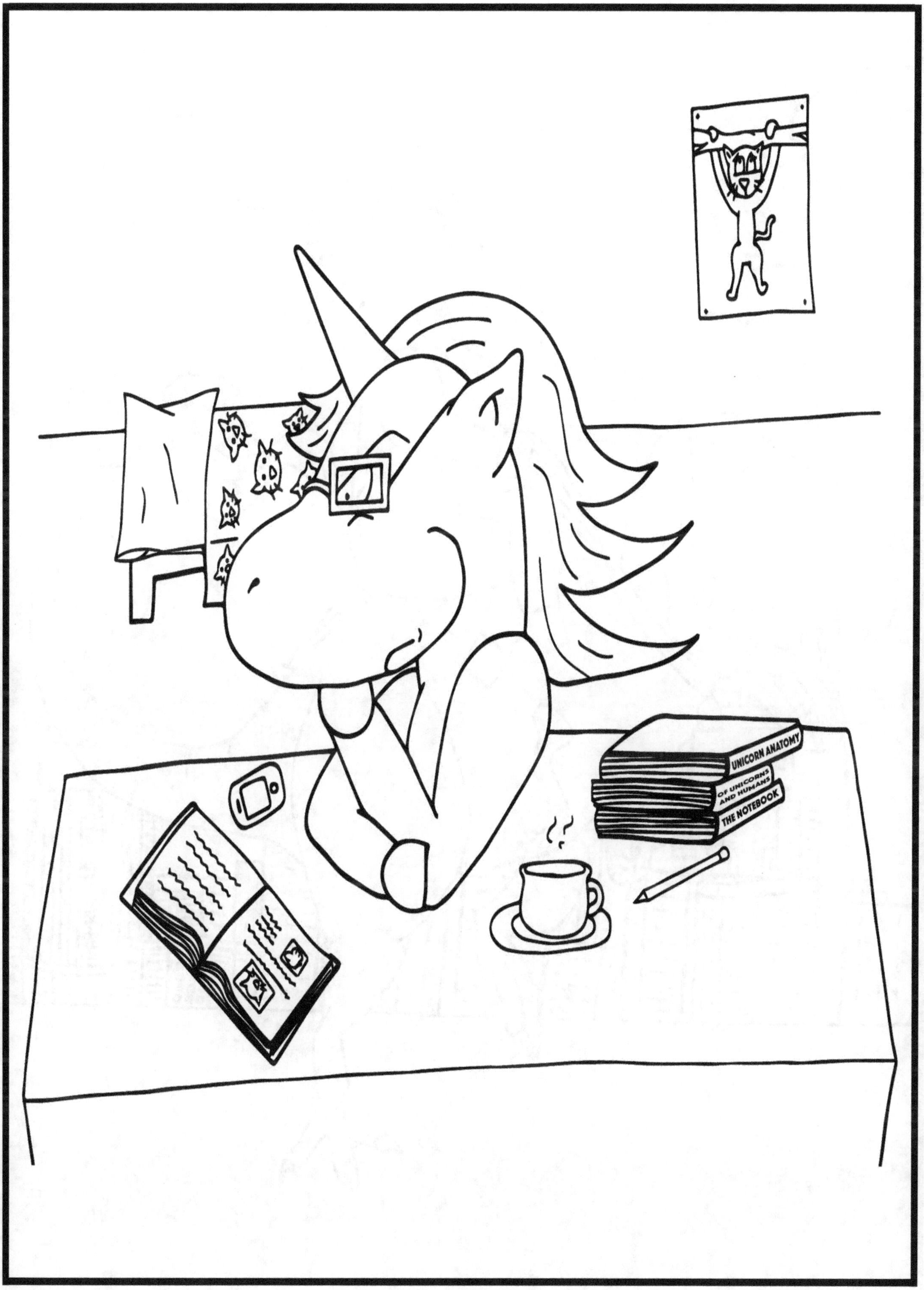
UNICORN ANATOMY
OF UNICORNS AND HUMANS
THE NOTEBOOK

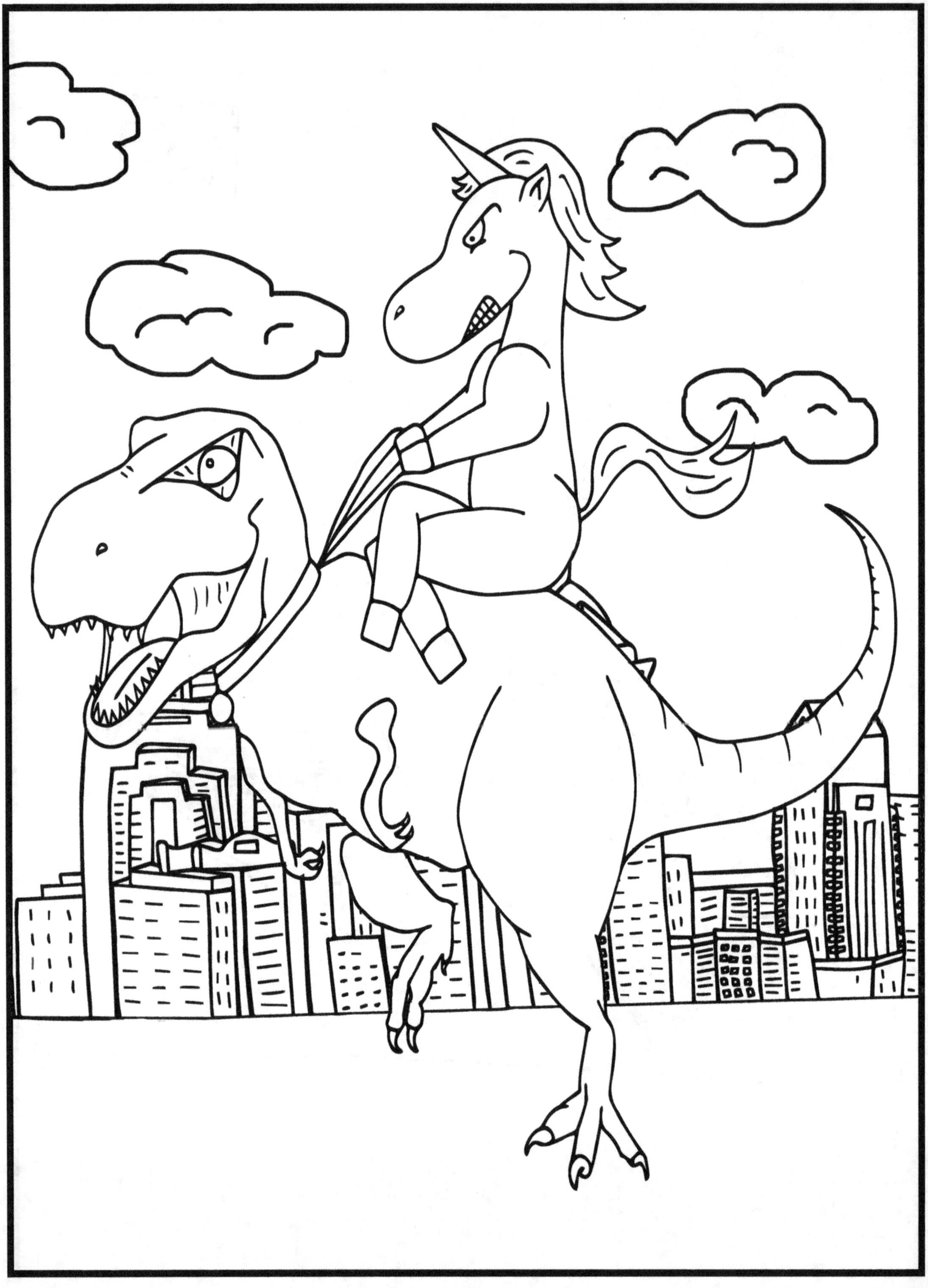

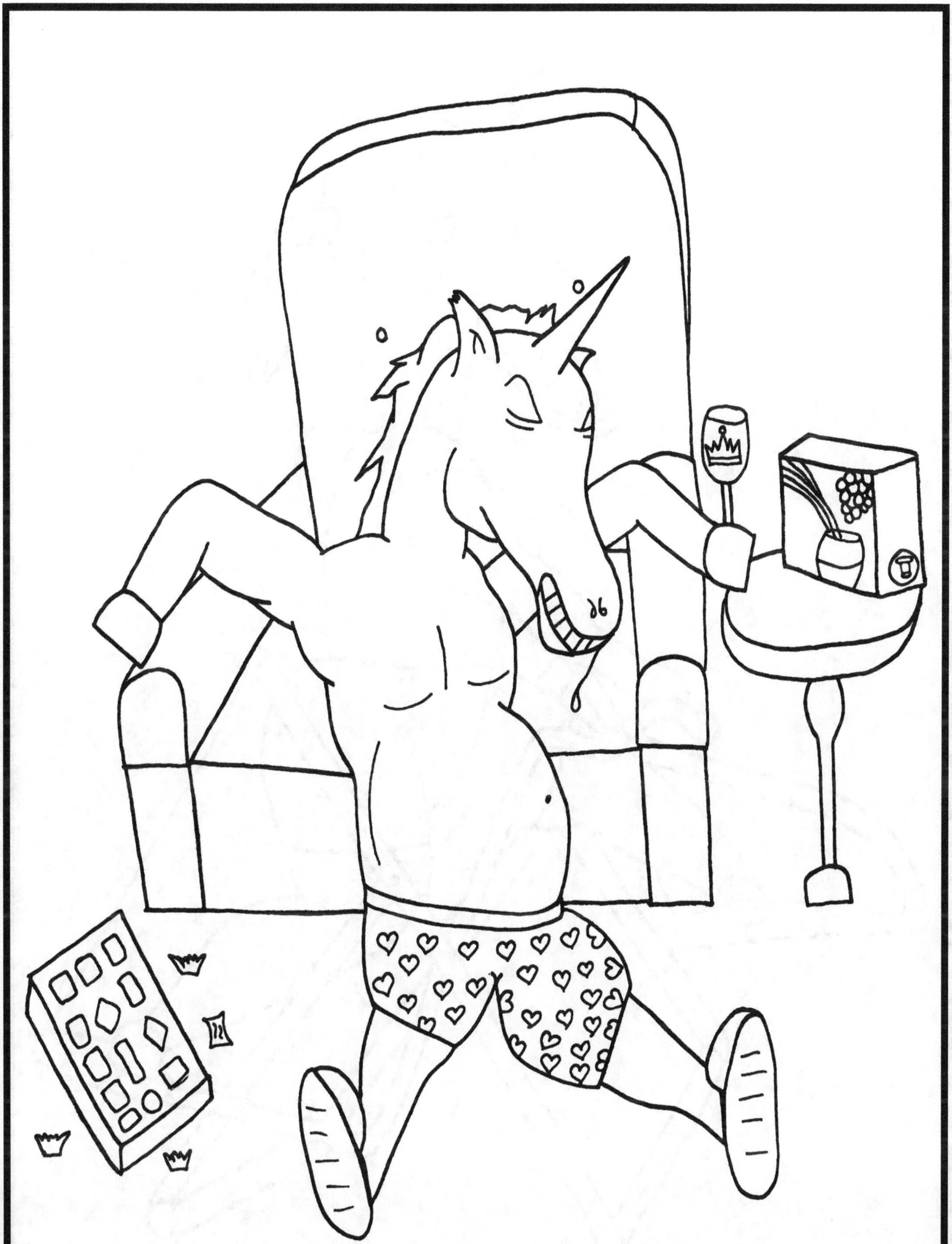

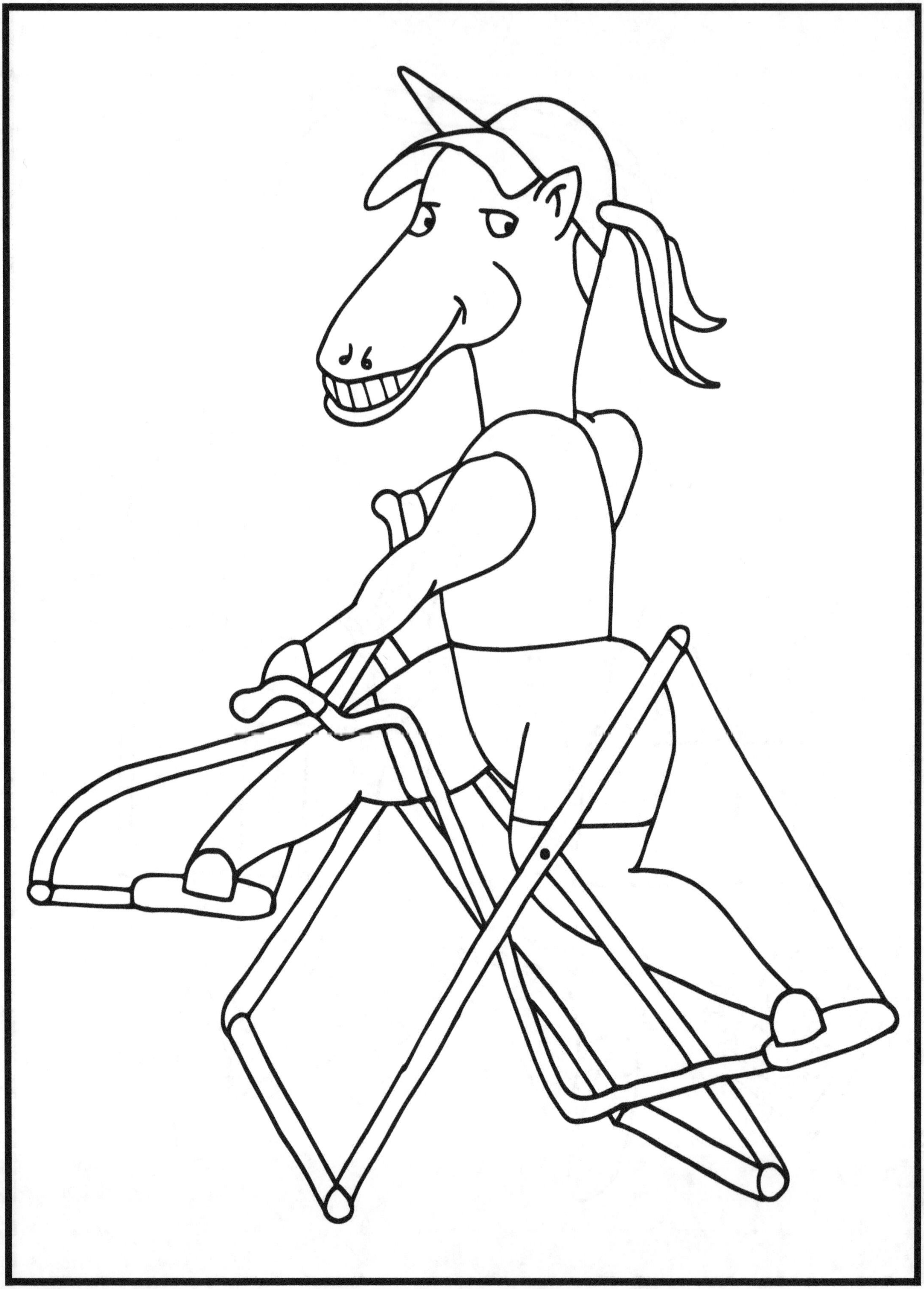

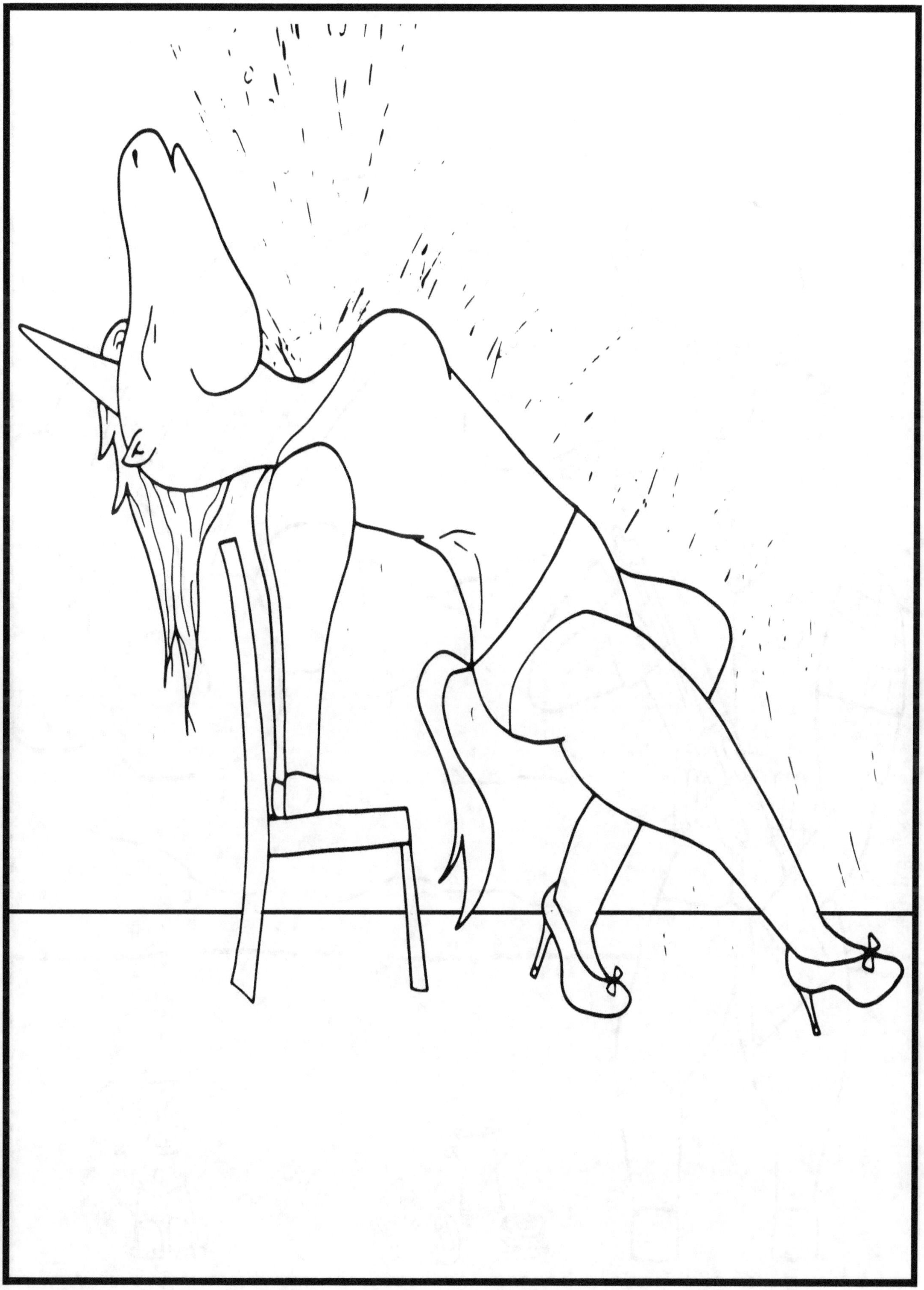

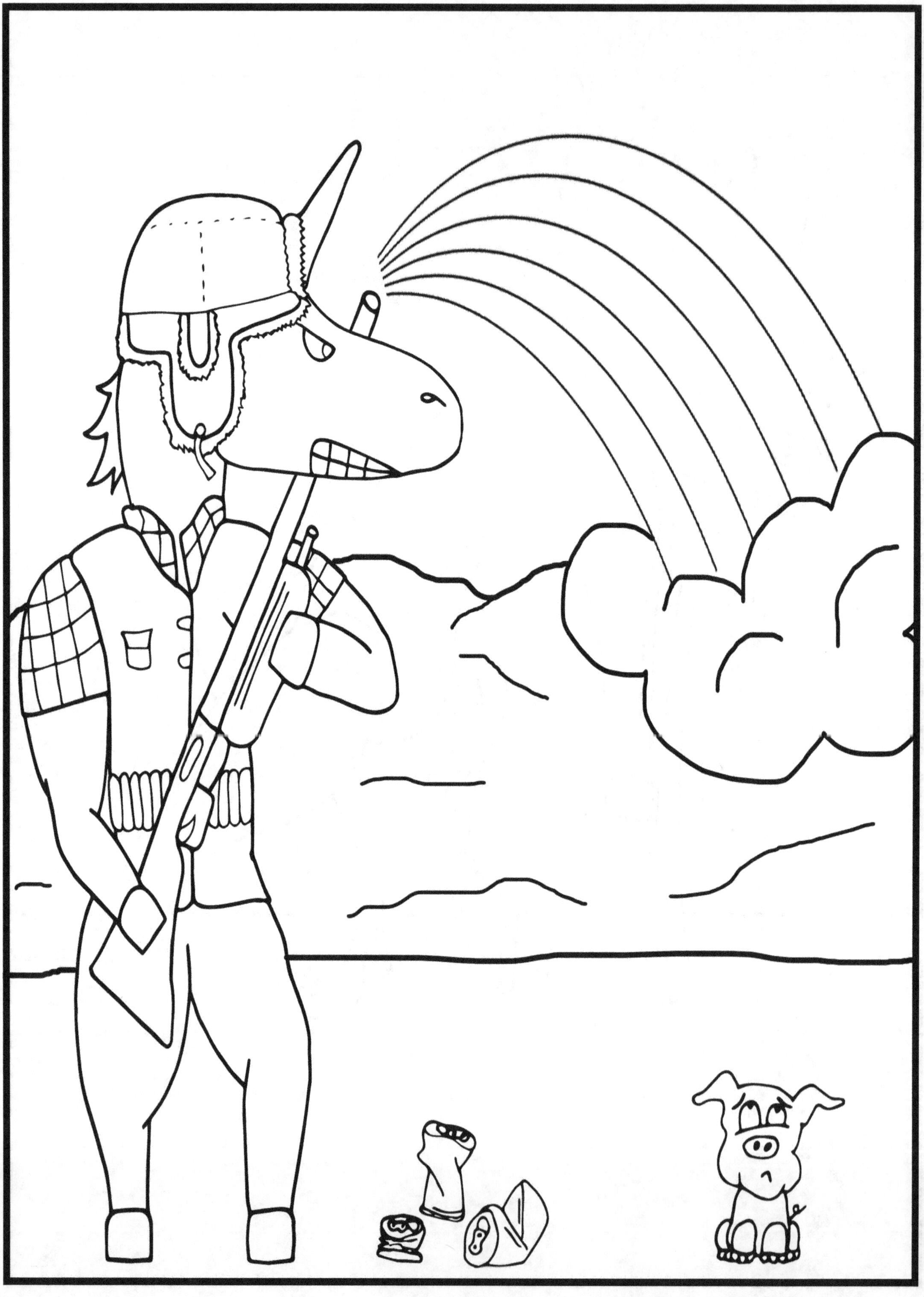

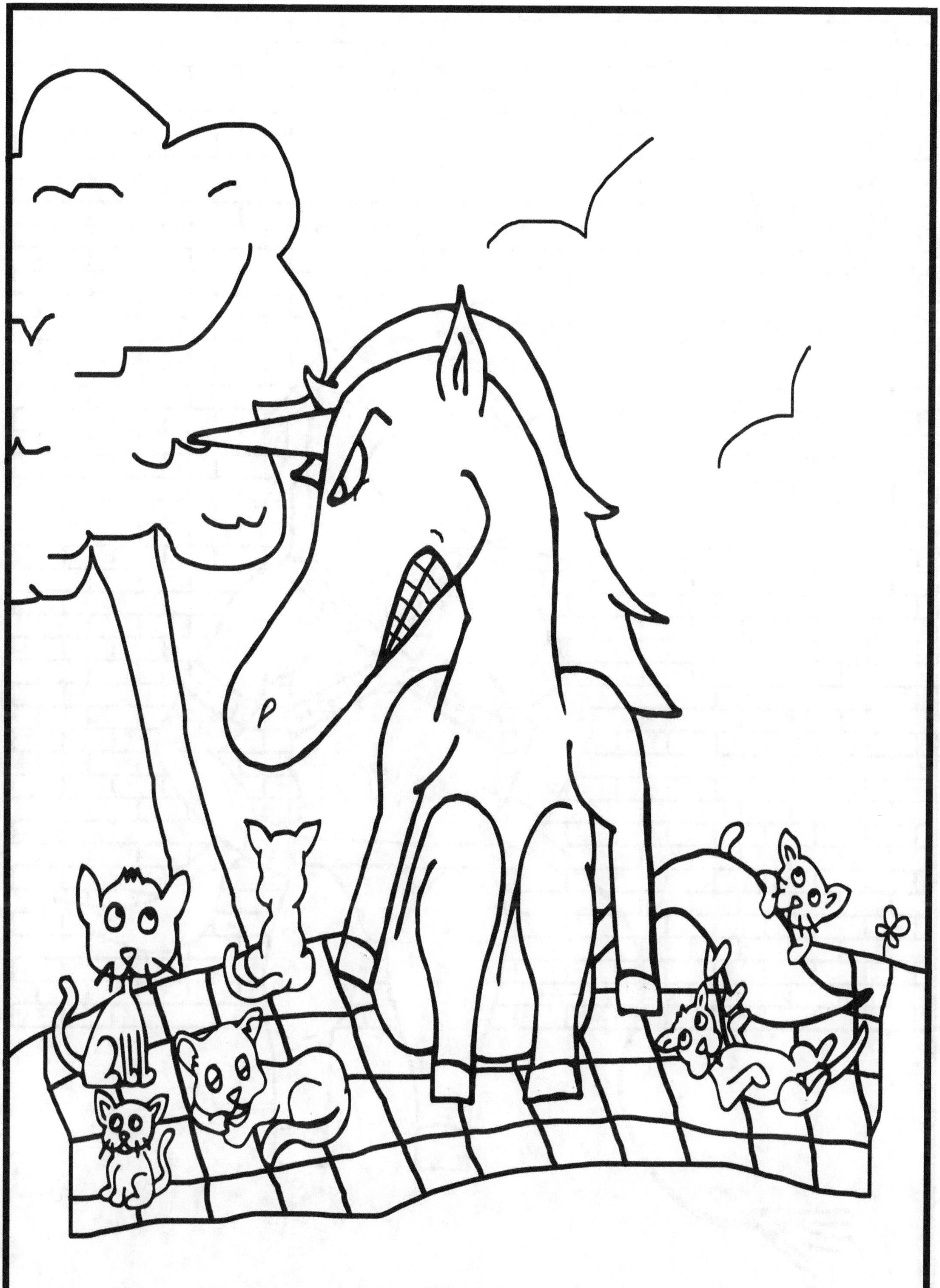

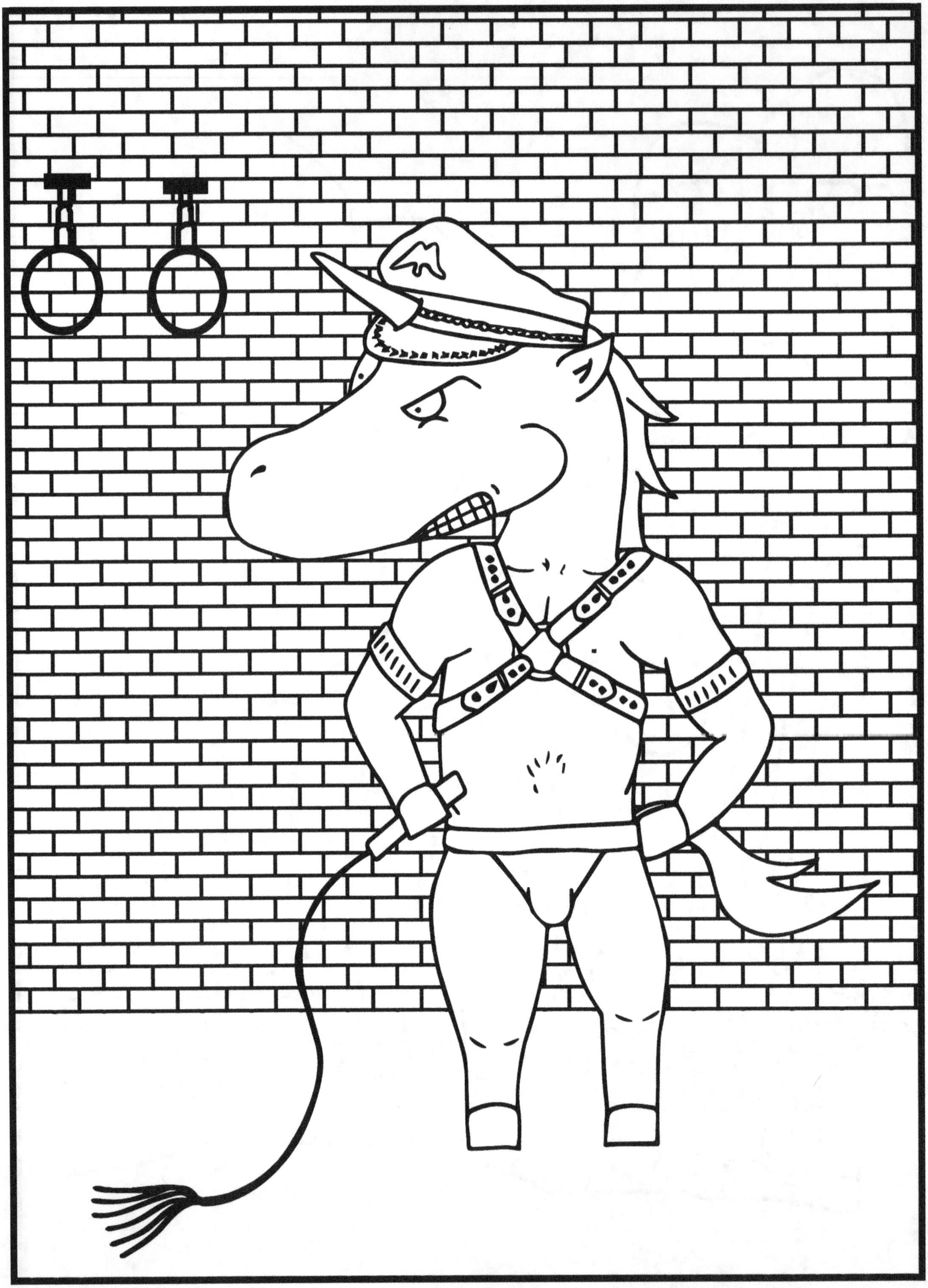

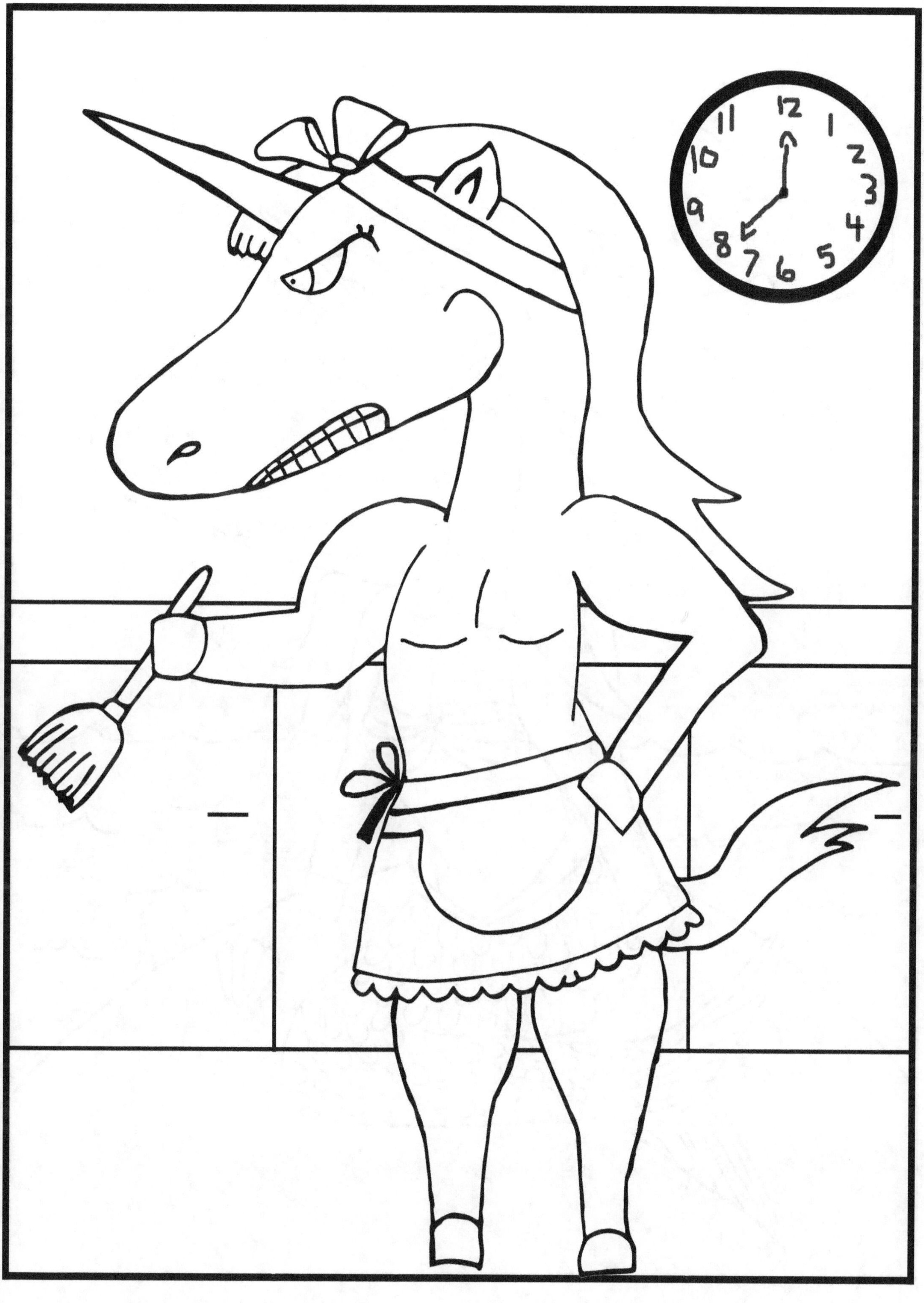
12
1
2
3
4
5
6
7
8
9
10
11

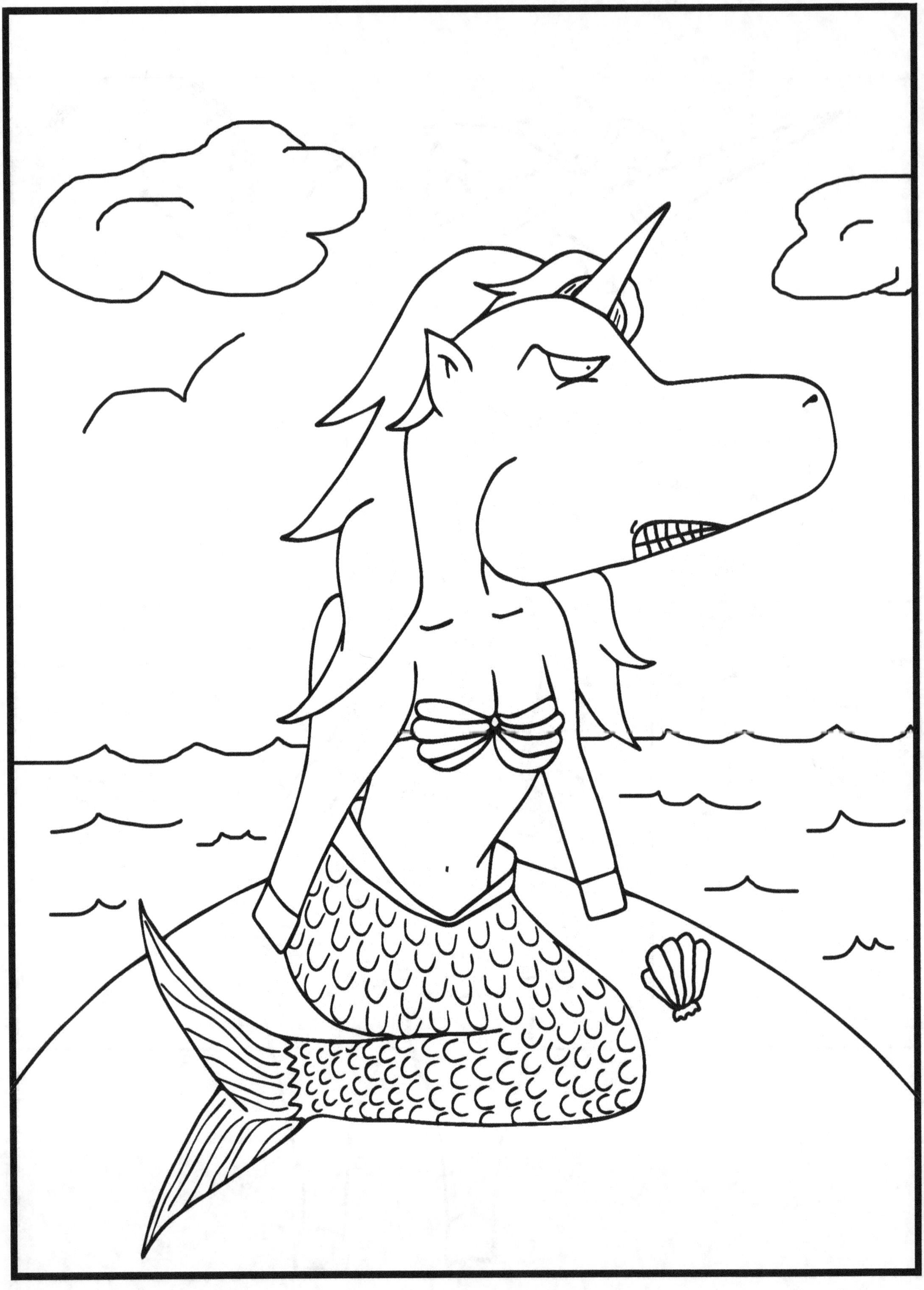

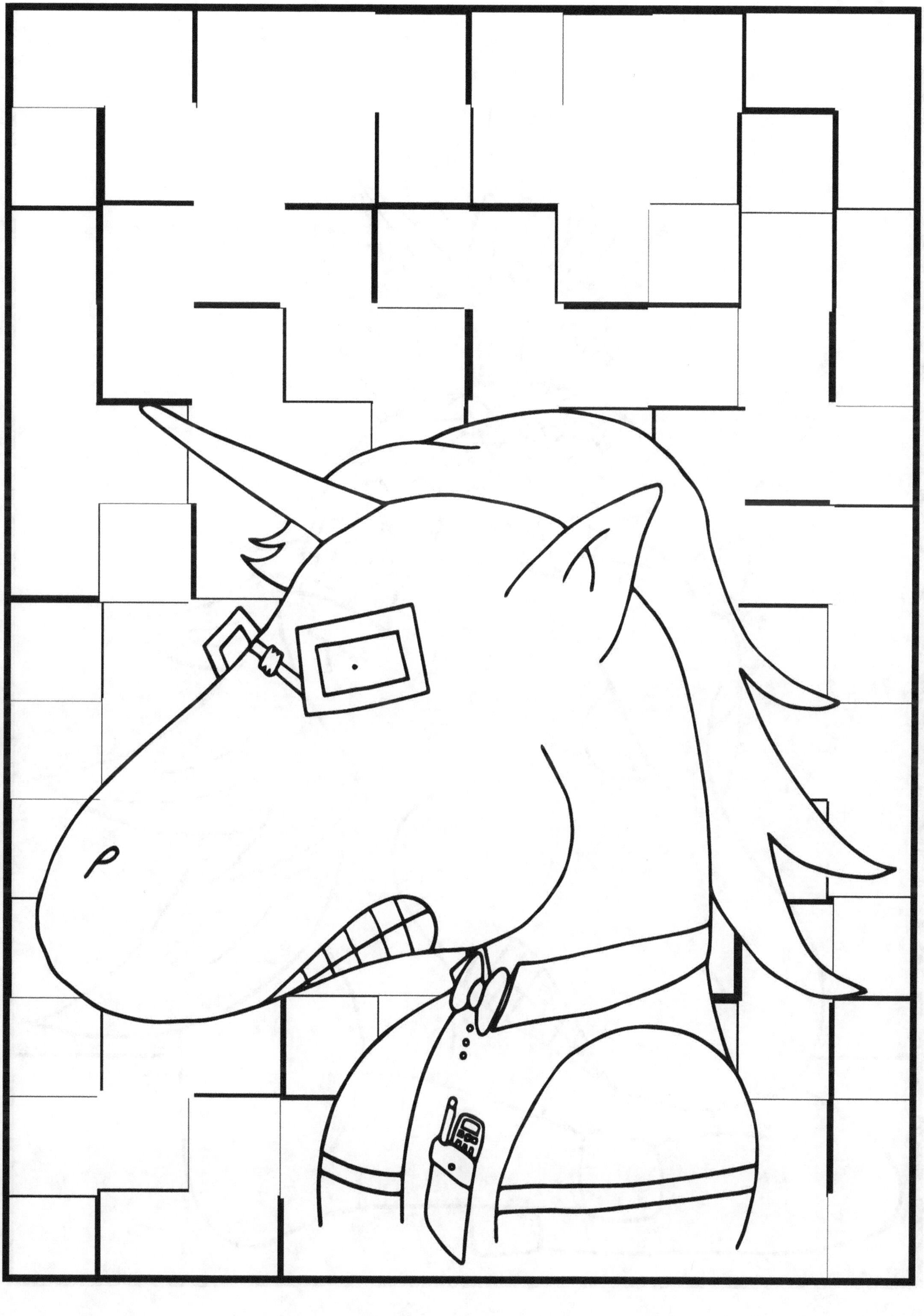

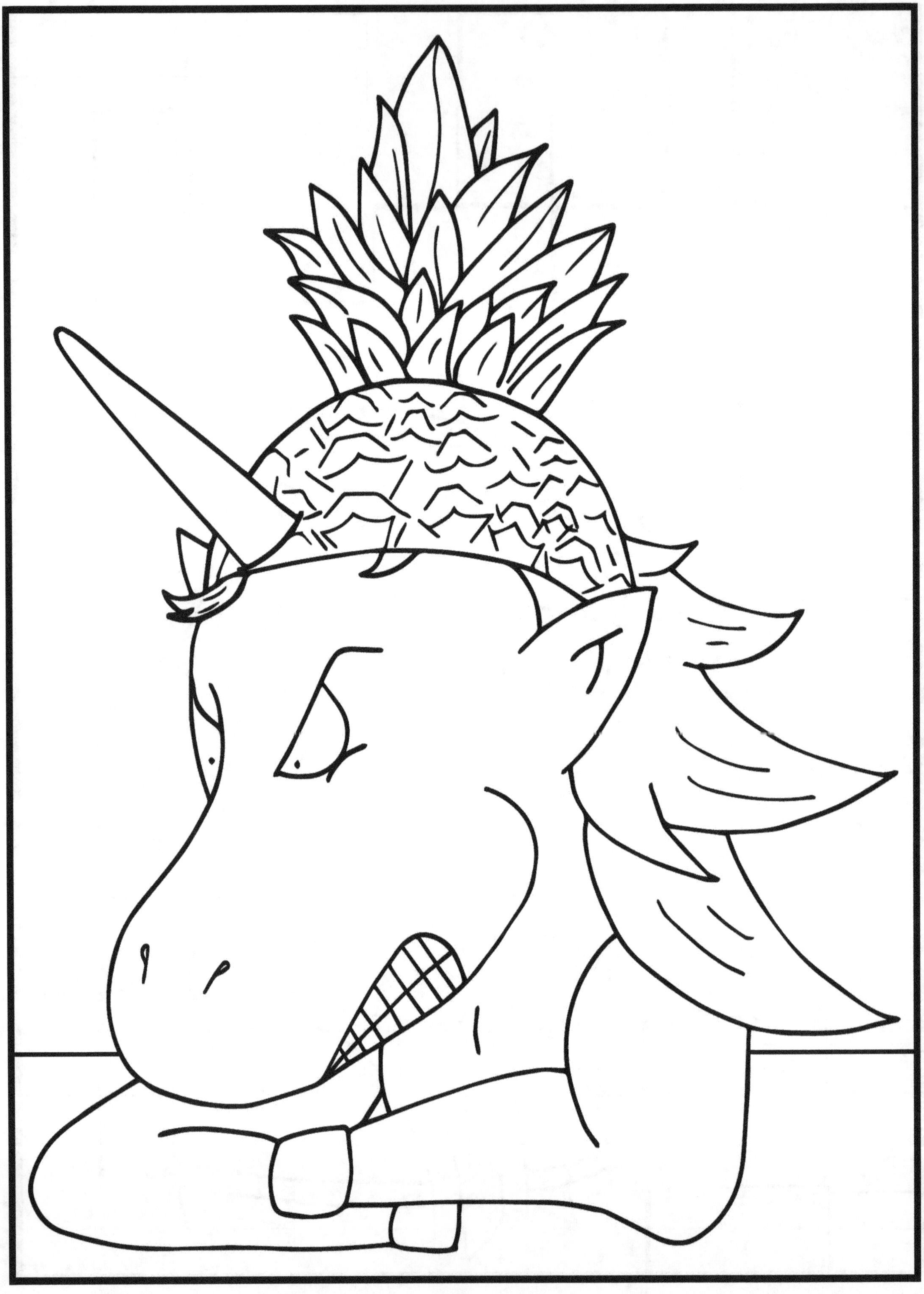

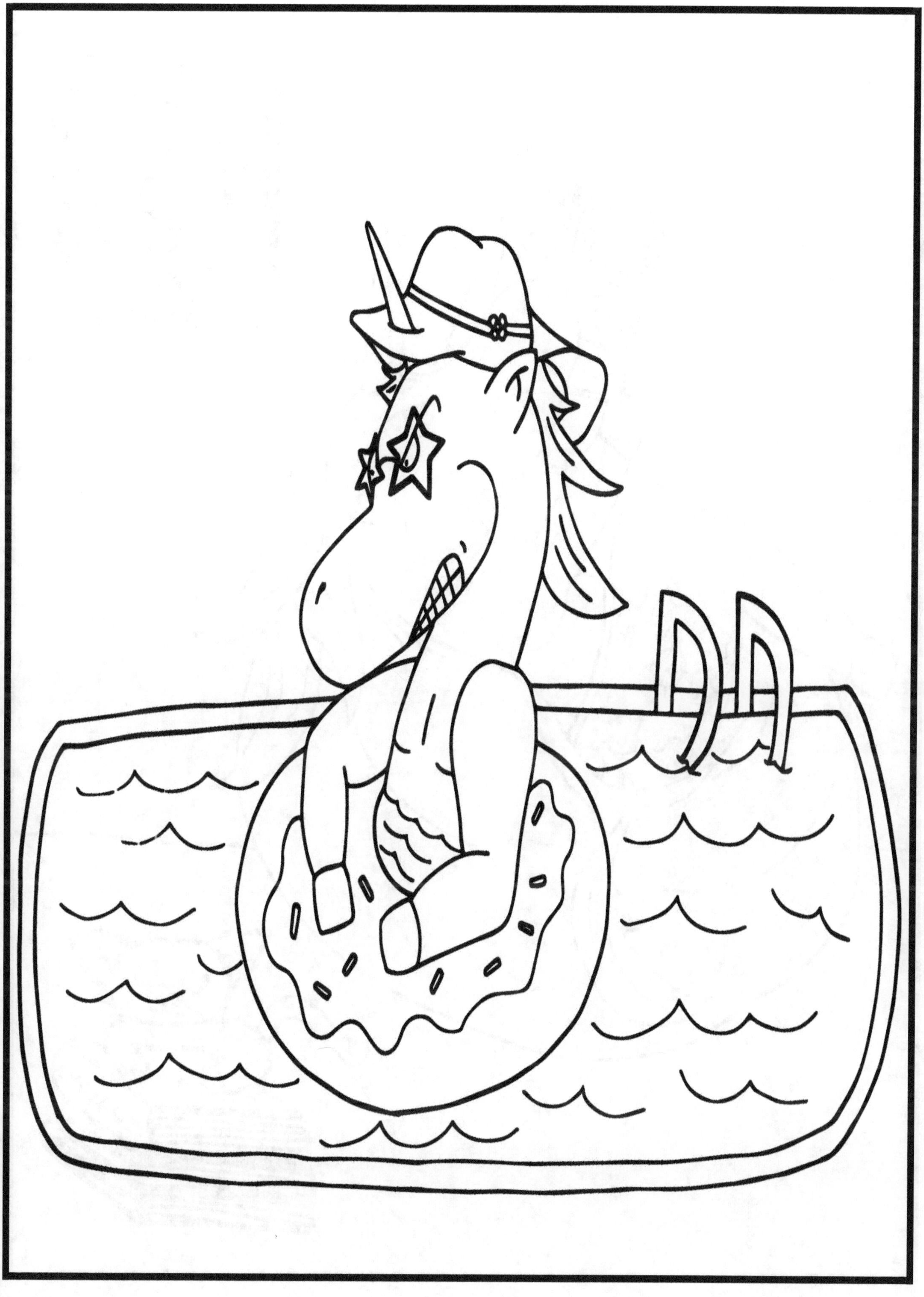

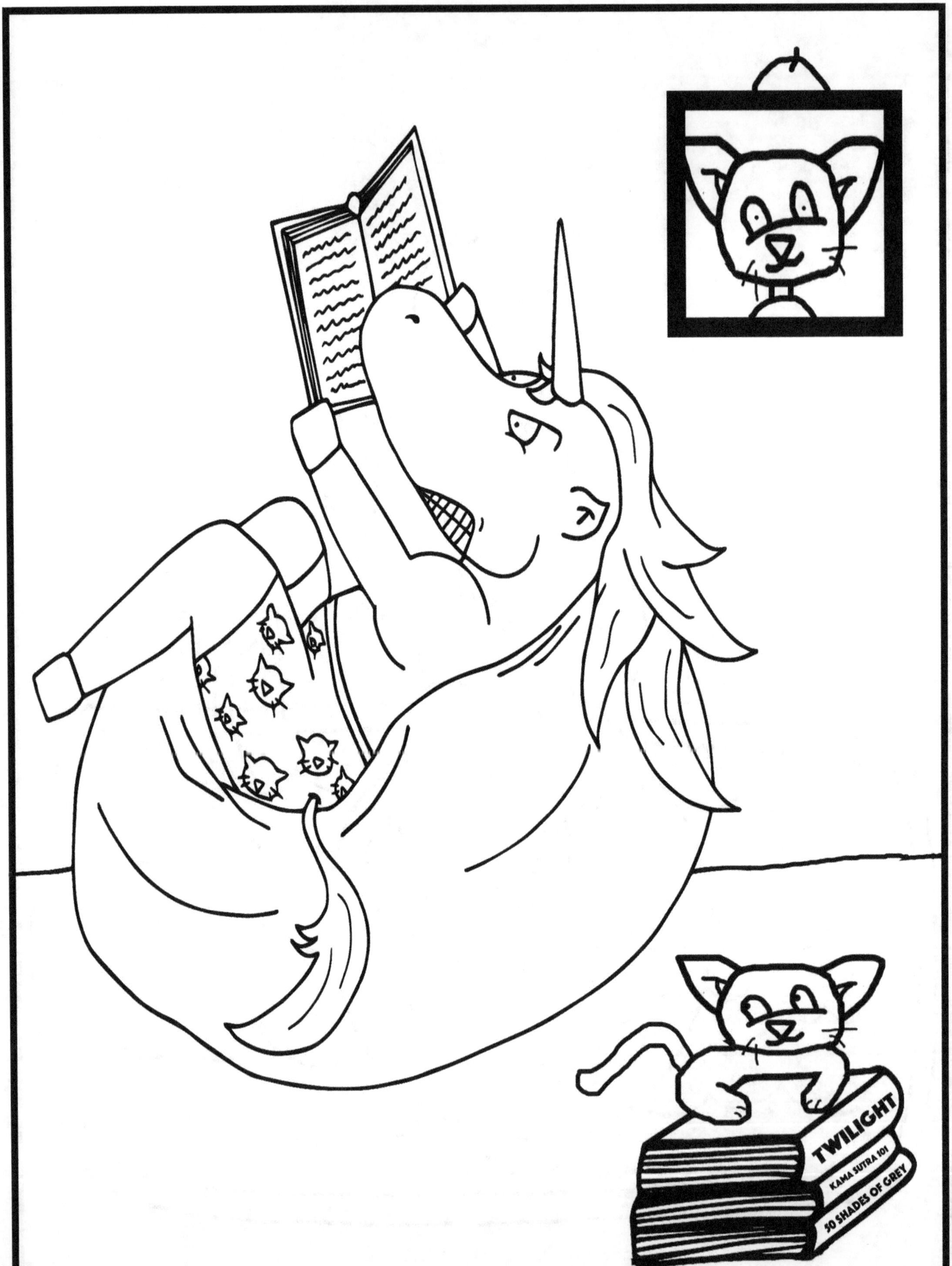
TWILIGHT
KAMA SUTRA 101
50 SHADES OF GREY

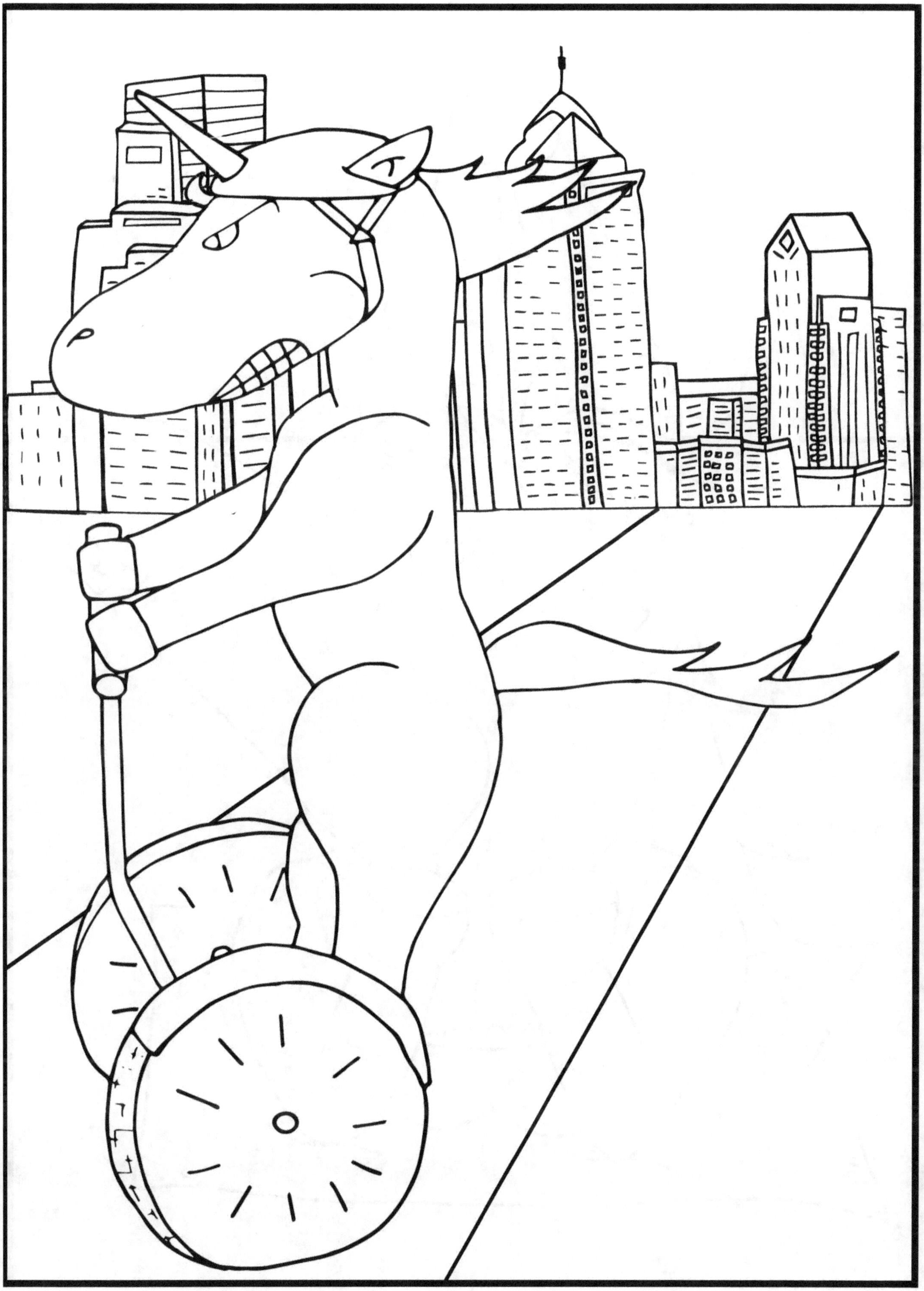

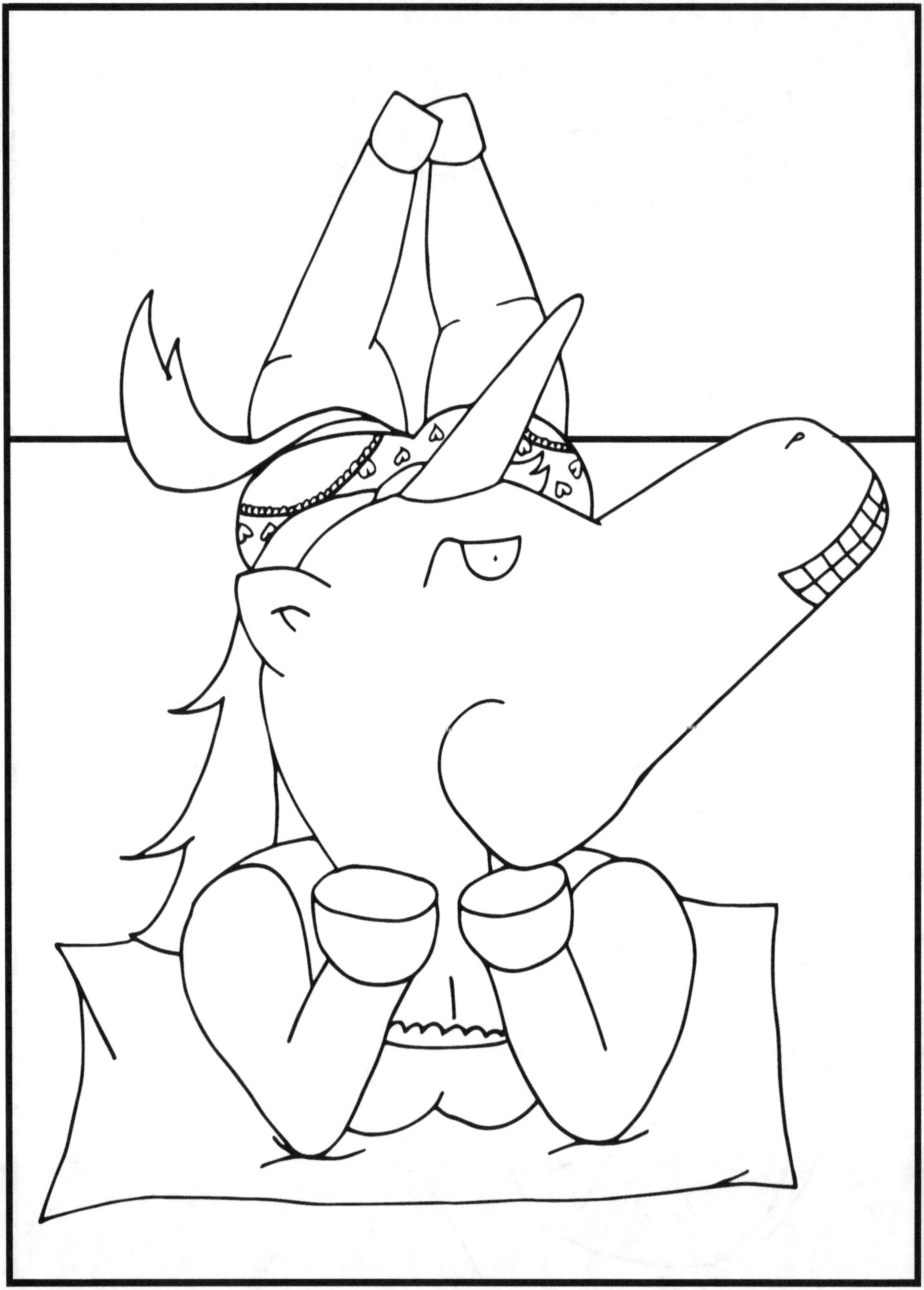

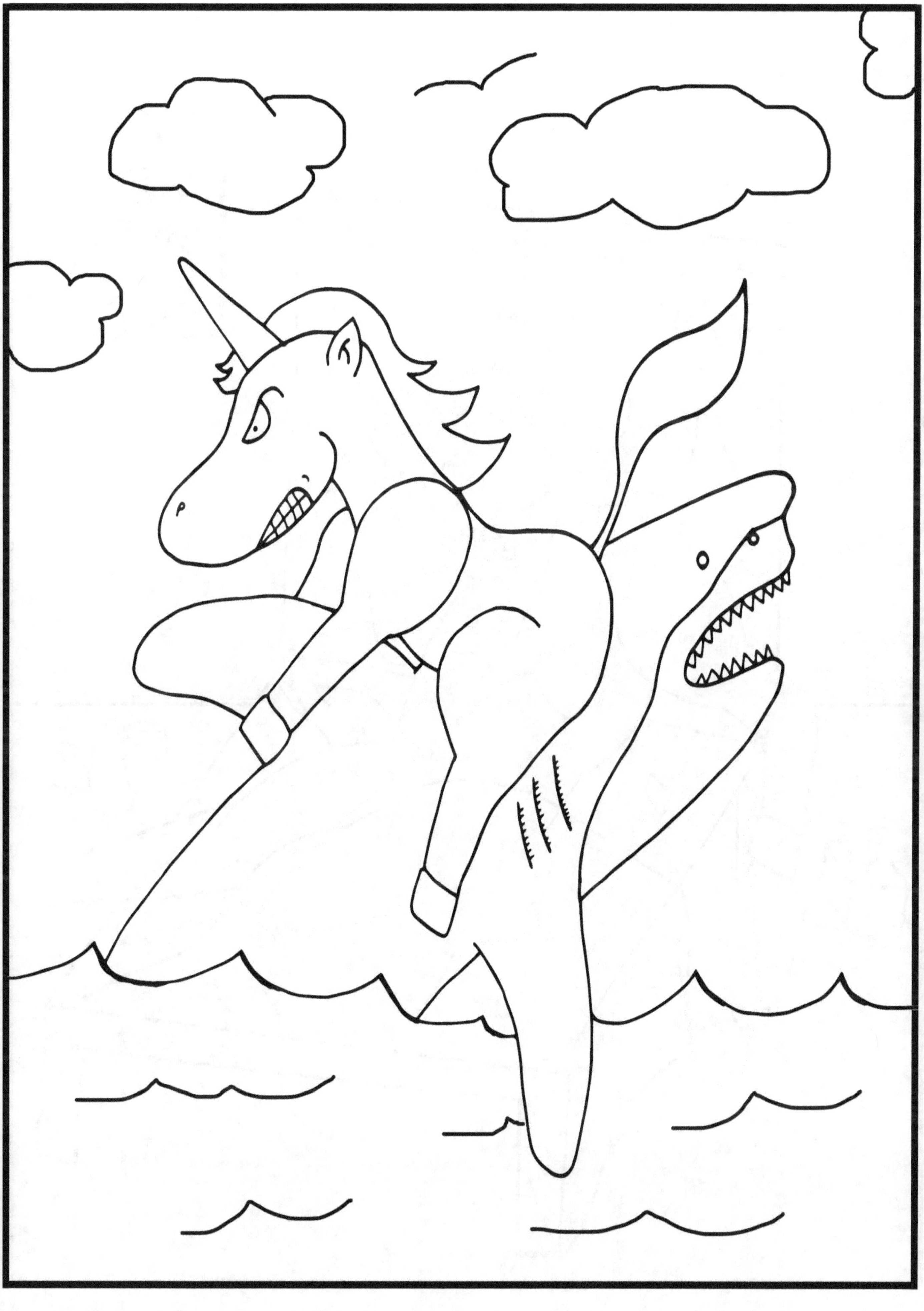

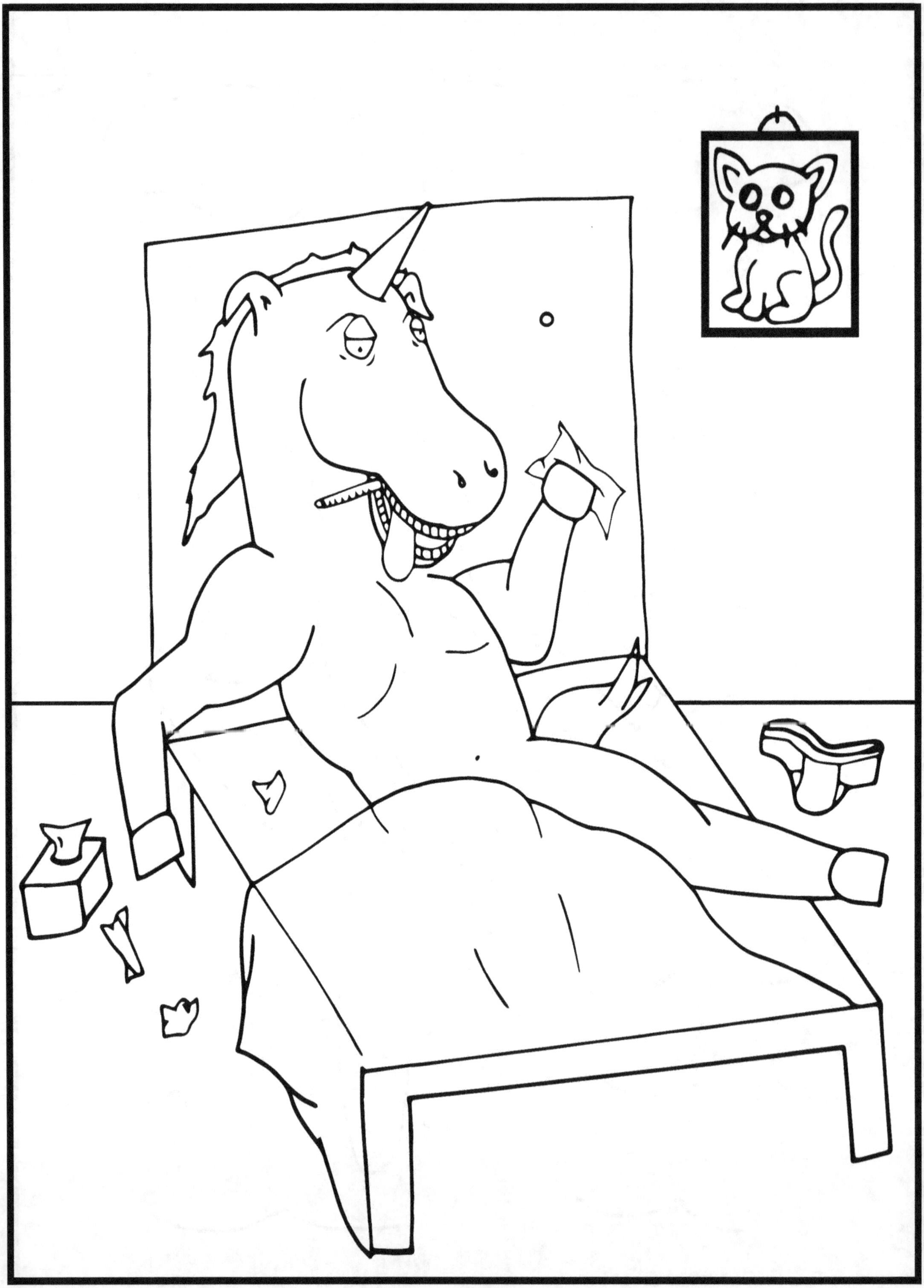

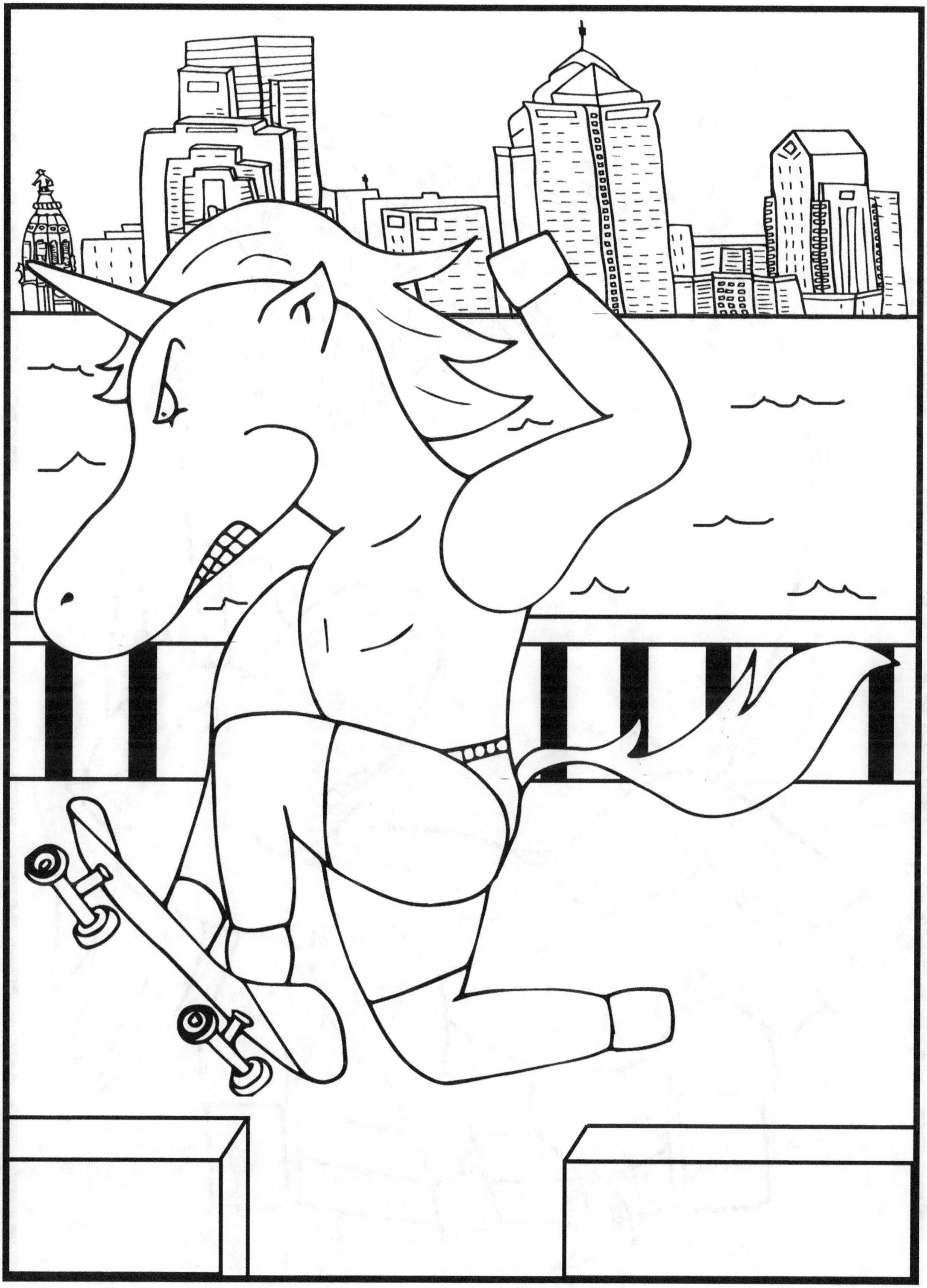

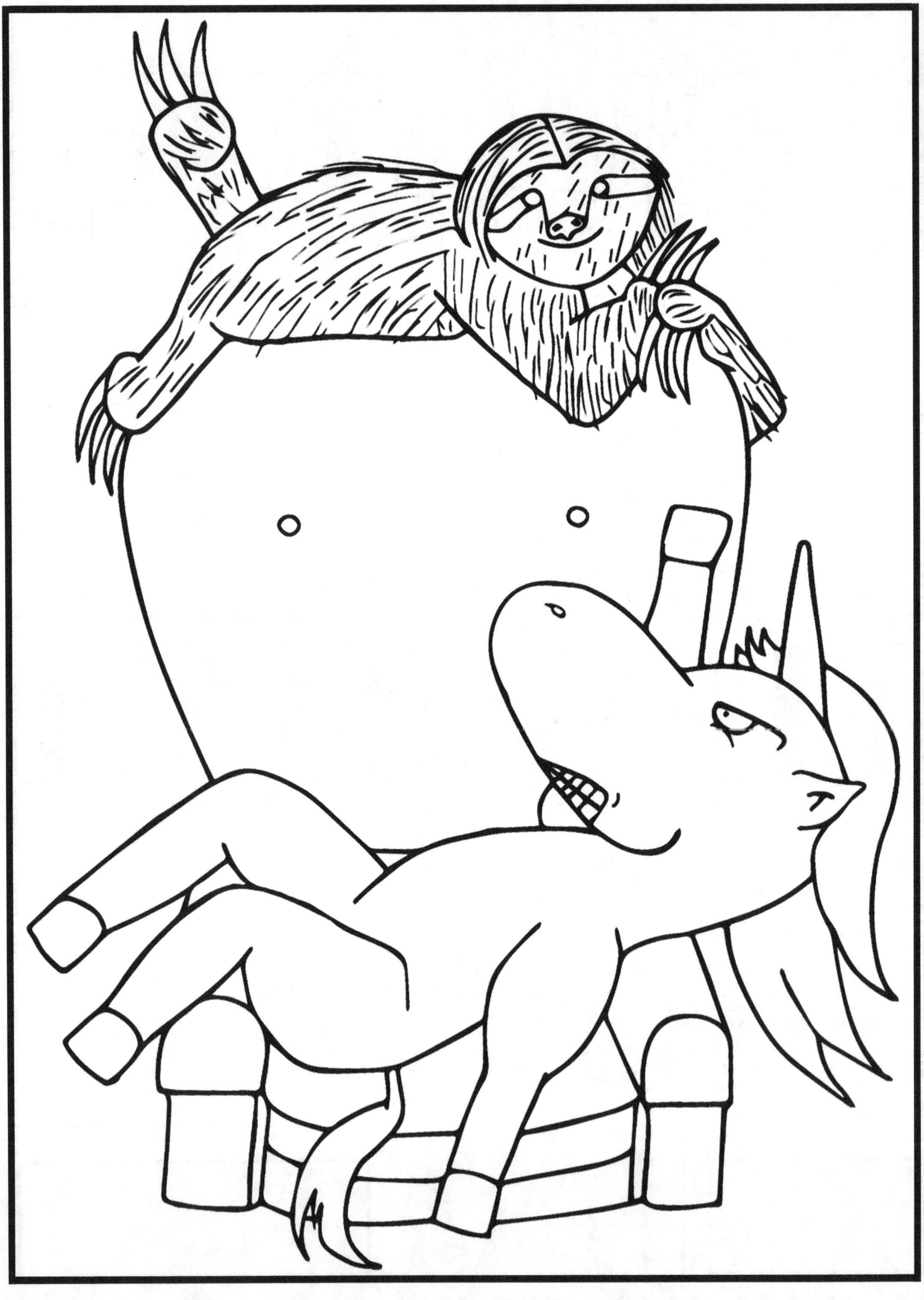

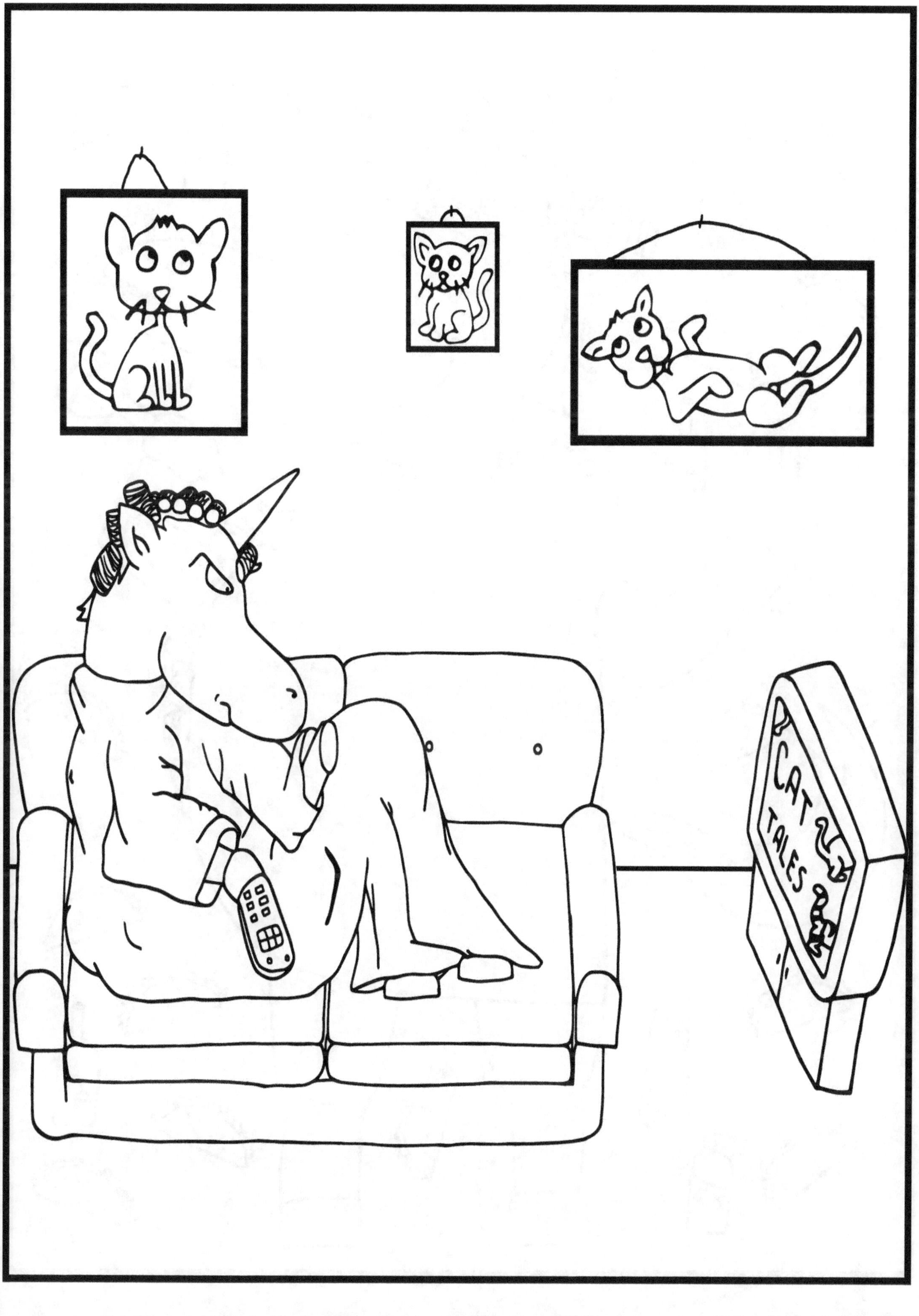
CAT
TALES

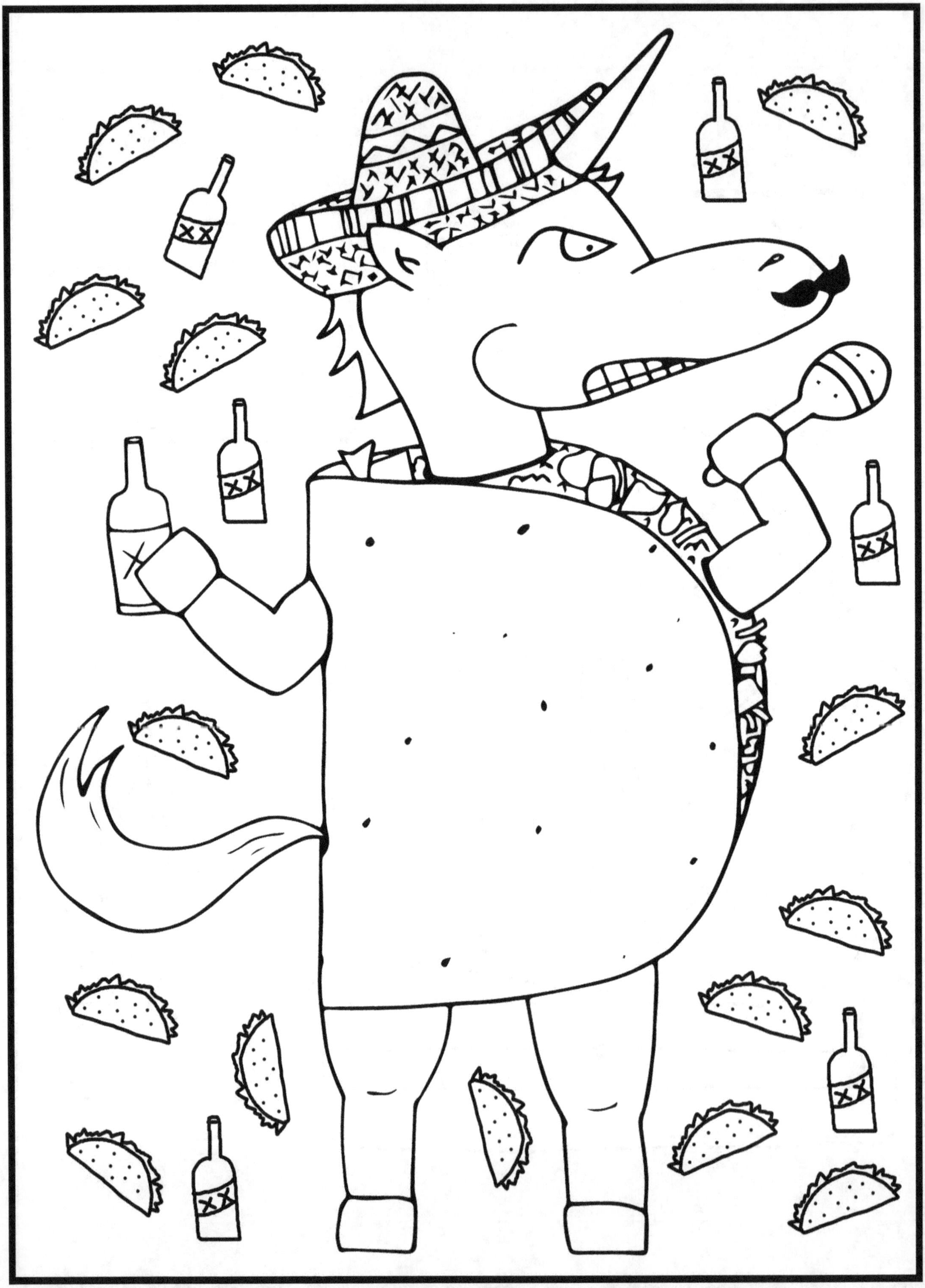

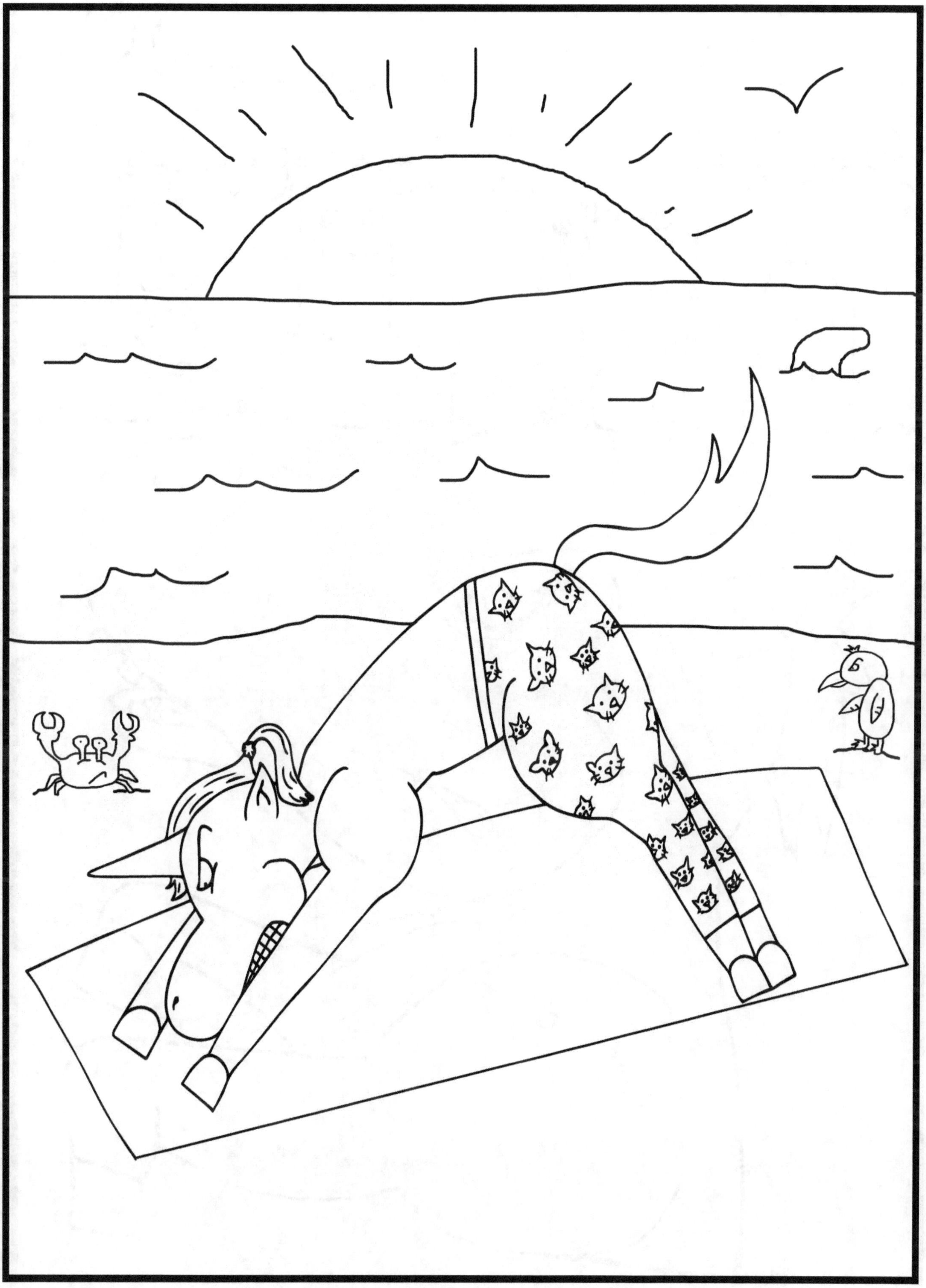

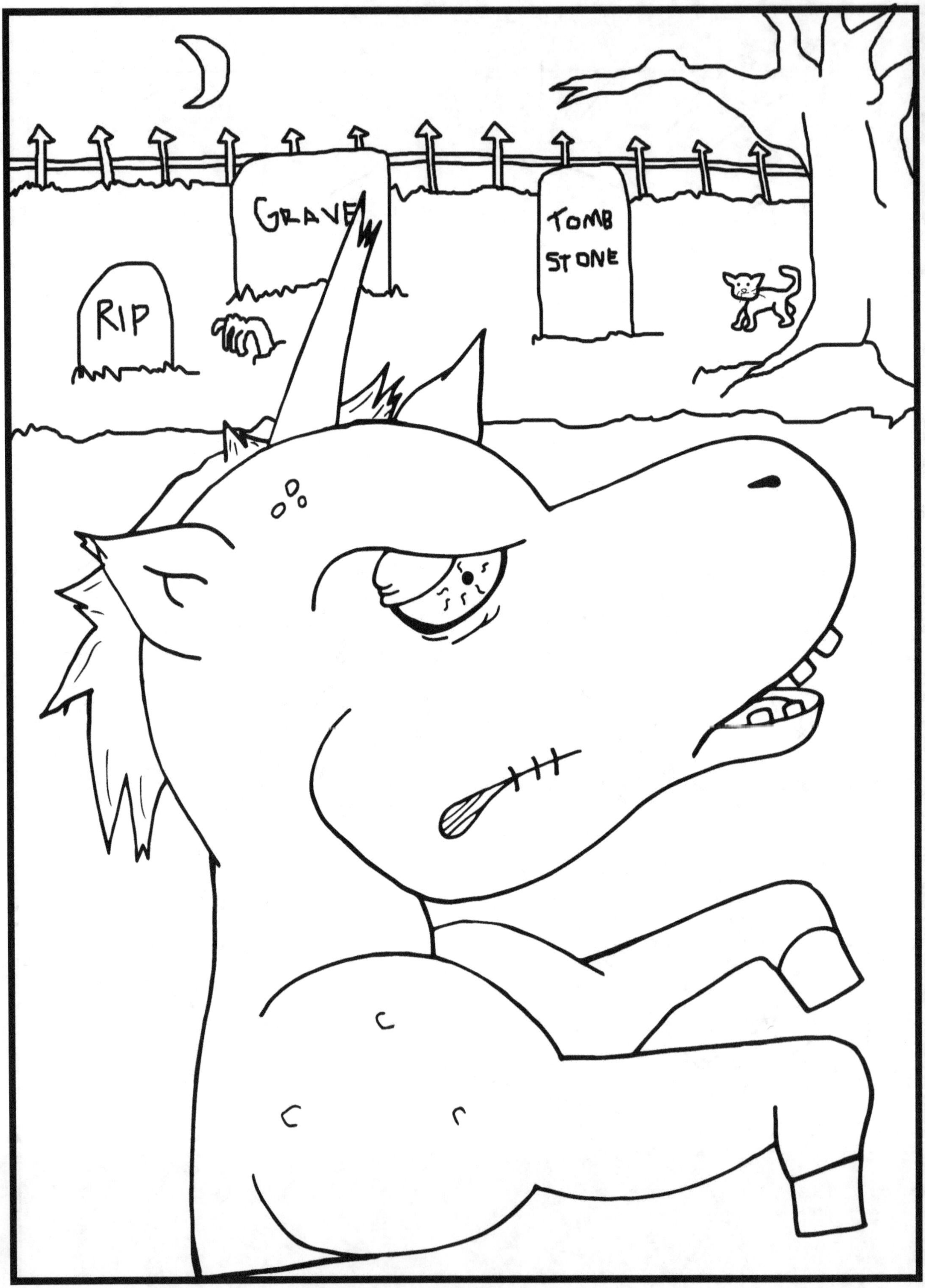
GRAVE
TOMB STONE
RIP

www.ingramcontent.com/pod-product-compliance
Lightning Source LLC
Chambersburg PA
CBHW080531190526
45169CB00008B/3116
* 9 7 8 1 5 3 7 0 5 1 5 4 3 *